5 Reasons

To Tell Your Boss To Go

F K Themselves!

HOW POSITIVE
PSYCHOLOGY CAN
HELP YOU **GET**
WHAT YOU WANT

Author's Note: The names and identifying details of some of the people portrayed in this book have been changed.

5 Reasons To Tell Your Boss To Go F**k Themselves: How Positive Psychology Can Help You Get What You Want.

Author: Michelle McQuaid
PO Box 230 Albert Park, VIC, 3206 Australia
ABN: 88094250503
www.michellemcquaid.com
Email: chelle@michellemcquaid.com

First published by Michelle McQuaid in 2012.
Typesetting: Rochelle Stone & That's Creative! Ebook Design.
Printed and bound in America by Create Space.
Distributed in America by Create Space.
www.createspace.com.

ISBN: 978-0-9872714-0-2

MICHELLE MCQUAID

5 Reasons

To Tell Your Boss To Go

F**K Themselves!

Contents

For Patrick, Megan, Kristy, Barb, Kym, Bridget, James and all the bad bosses we've ever had (you know who you are!).

And for Jim Stynes, whose passion and courage inspired me to reach for the stars. You are dearly missed my friend.

Preface

My boss was a big man, both in stature and status. He was renowned for yelling so loudly, and so often, his office had been moved to the far end of the building so fewer people would be traumatized by his daily rants.

"You're on," said his executive assistant, sticking her head into my office with a sympathetic smile. Oh joy! My performance review meeting had arrived.

I was particularly dreading it this year. You see, a few months ago I'd burst into tears at work and my boss had quickly made up his mind that I wasn't resilient enough. Mortified, I put it down to the hormonal swirl of early pregnancy. But my boss was now certain that I was much too sensitive, so he'd assigned an executive coach to toughen me up. Ah crap!

As the coaching kicked in, I tried to dismiss my misgivings. After all, putting up with some rubbish is part of every job. Just check: it's in the fine print of your employment contract (well, almost).

After a couple of sessions, the coach decided that my resilience was just fine, but my boss couldn't be convinced, so he instituted spot checks. "So, have you toughened up yet?" he'd bark, at the top of his lungs, every time we met.

As the weeks turned into months and his campaign to toughen me up persisted, I began to be filled with self-doubt. What if he was right? What if I really wasn't tough enough? What if I'd only gotten this far by sheer luck?

Worried that my job was on the line, I resorted to trying to be someone that I'm not. I tried to prove my hard-heartedness by giving colleagues a difficult time and taking unreasonably tough stands. I was a nightmare. I started dreading going to work and it reflected in my performance on the job.

It wasn't just at the office that the costs were mounting up. I was lying awake at night worrying about what to do next. I'd stopped exercising because I felt too exhausted. I was lonely because my friends were sick of hearing me complain about work. And I felt terribly ashamed that all of my joy for life seemed to have been swept away because of this one man.

Everything seemed to be spiraling down, down, down to dust. There had to be a way to turn this around. What would it take to make this right?

Having completed my Masters in Positive Psychology, I understood only too well how excessive negativity can wreak havoc in our lives. I'd become so fixated on all the things I hated about my boss, that I'd lost all perspective about what it was I actually wanted from my job. And, without these positive images to keep pulling me forward, I'd gotten stuck in an endless loop of hopelessness.

I realized I didn't have to obsess about what I despised; I could put my attention elsewhere and start focusing on what I wanted from my job and the relationship with my boss. So, this first step toward transforming a bad boss situation of "getting real about what we're telling ourselves," which I outline in Chapter 1, allowed me to start shifting my beliefs – just enough – to see a glimpse of hope that maybe all wasn't lost.

Taking back control

I'd also resigned myself to the fact that I was completely helpless – after all, he was my boss. But to be honest, that was only half the story. My boss may have initiated our difficulties, but the dirty looks and snide remarks I'd since retaliated with proved that I wasn't completely powerless. Maybe I couldn't do anything about his fixation on my resilience, but I could do something about my reaction to the way he was handling it.

I wasn't ready to call it quits yet, but I did want to be able to come to work and get on with my job and for this resilience rubbish to stop. I wanted to be empowered to make good decisions happen so that I could feel proud of my work. And I wanted a relationship that was based on trust and mutual respect with my boss, yet my recent behavior had moved me towards a very different place.

Having accepted that maybe my boss wasn't completely to blame for what had been going on, I was curious about why a reasonable, rational, but inherently flawed human being (like most of us) would behave in such a way. I needed to make sense of his obsession with my resilience if I was going to find a constructive way of repairing our relationship so that I could happily get on with my job.

In my studies of cognitive psychology and, ironically, resilience, I'd learnt that we all have a little voice in our head that is constantly whispering our darkest fears – particularly in the moments that most try us. My voice whispers, "You're not really good enough," and it was a big piece of why my boss' campaign had triggered such a bad reaction in me. I wondered what my boss' voice was whispering for him to behave in such an extreme manner.

I dug back into my psychology books to rediscover the connections between our beliefs and our behaviors. My boss' temper was so famous that it was easy to connect his anger with its trigger belief that his rights were somehow being violated. Perhaps it was that he resented my teary outburst for fear that it reflected badly on his leadership and so was now relentlessly focused on my resilience to ensure I wouldn't embarrass him ever again.

I'll never know how accurate my diagnosis was, but this small insight into the things that could be driving my boss reminded me that he probably wasn't that bad a person; in this case he was just doing a very bad job. I didn't feel forgiveness – his ongoing demands for toughness were still too raw – but I did feel a little empathy and a lot more confidence that I could manage around his behavior.

A little help from my friends

By now, work had started to feel just a little easier and this second step, which I unveil in Chapter 2, of "owning our own story so we're ready to act," motivated me to start experimenting with ways to improve the situation with my boss.

Feeling a little more optimistic about my future, I was finally able to reach out to a close friend and come clean about how ashamed I'd been feeling as a result of what was happening with my boss. She listened to my shame with complete empathy and connected with the sense of pain that had paralyzed me for so long. Then, she asked me what I was going to do next given work was still pretty shitty due to the constant resilience battle being waged.

"Honestly, I wish I could tell him that with the greatest respect he can just go fuck himself," I said. She was so shocked at my language (my mother would have scrubbed my mouth out with soap) that she started to laugh – and so did I. My god, it felt good to laugh again. I hadn't laughed with abandon in the longest time. My amusement ensured that a spiral of positivity started bubbling up.

"So, why don't you?" my friend asked. Yeah right! Can you imagine how loudly he'd yell about that? They'd hear him all the way down to accounts on the next floor!

But, as the days passed by, I couldn't get the idea out of my head. And every time I tried to imagine the conversation, I couldn't help but laugh. So, although I loathed the possibility of being yelled at and was seriously worried that I'd be officially reprimanded or thrown out, I decided that if I could hold my intention lightly – to respectfully ask him to give up on the toughness boot camp – it just might work. Besides, things couldn't go on as they were. I wasn't willing to start spiraling down into darkness again just because of my boss.

Finding win-win outcomes

My performance review was imminent and the issue of my resilience would certainly be raised so it seemed the perfect time to make my request. So, having completed the third step I outline in Chapter 3 of "connecting with others to create win-win outcomes," I was ready to face my boss.

"Come in. Take a seat," said my boss with a smile, as I slid into his glass office.

My boss had been well trained. He began my review with some good feedback about my performance this year. Nice. But then, we soon moved onto the real fun.

"So, how's your resilience going, do you feel like you've toughened up?" he asked, doing his best to look supportive.

I took a long, slow breath so that I was completely calm, looked him square in the eyes and softened my face with a very slight smile. "Well," I said as casually as I could, "At this point, with the greatest respect, when it comes to my resilience you can go fuck yourself."

He looked at me and there was deathly silence.

I'd chosen my words very carefully. I wanted him to feel safe, not under attack, hence my use of the phrase "with the greatest respect". I didn't want to trigger off that voice in his head that his rights were somehow being violated.

But, I also wanted him to know that I was confident, capable and courageous enough to ask for what I needed. He had never heard me say the word "fuck" and I knew it'd shock him into giving me his full attention.

I'd also chosen my tone quite deliberately. There was a slight sound of levity around the heaviness of my words to ensure that while the situation was taken seriously, the people involved treated each other lightly. And I was hoping like hell he'd reciprocate.

Several seconds had passed and he was still looking at me and I dared not look away, so I sat there quietly waiting.

Slowly the corners of his mouth started to turn up. Then he let out a bellow – a laugh, not a yell – and shook his head. "Fair enough, I guess," he said, "Fair enough."

Then, I quietly, but firmly spoke my truth.

"I feel that my resilience is just fine and I'd like us to move on rather than dwelling on it any longer if that's alright," I qualified, so that my request was clear.

And then just like that, we moved on to other matters and my resilience was never spoken of again. Yay!

With my confidence restored, work soon became enjoyable once more. My stress levels completely dropped away, regular sleep and exercise resumed and I happily spent time with my friends talking about things other than work. My sense of joy and serenity for life returned anew.

My performance rating and bonus were lower that year, which was chalked up to some "hiccups" in my performance rather than anything I said to my boss. To be honest, I didn't care because the sense of empowerment and self-respect I gained from that conversation was worth any cost. As it transpired, there was great peace and satisfaction in the fourth step I explain in Chapter 9, of "realizing that the best revenge is happiness."

Funnily enough, my boss also didn't look so big to me anymore. In fact, he looked like an ordinary guy who was often lost or overwhelmed by his apparent fear of being hurt. So much so, that he ran around making lots of noise and trying to bully others along because he didn't know how to manage his own emotions. Poor fella – wouldn't want to be stuck inside his head!

Paying it forward

Most surprising of all though, was that when I shared this story with friends, other horror stories of bad bosses came pouring out. Apparently, they were everywhere.

There were control-freak bosses trying to fix us, incompetent bosses who undermined us, manipulative bosses who isolated us from others, narcissist bosses who cared nothing about us and moody bosses who got off on bullying us.

And none of us knew what to do about it.

For light relief, as we shared our tales of woe, we started responding with the rallying cry: "Ah, tell them to go fuck themselves!" And the very idea made us laugh every time. There was something about this phrase, perhaps its somewhat shocking playfulness, which helped to suck away the creeping terrors of our bad bosses so that the light of miraculous possibilities could shine.

Before you write us off entirely, you should know that studies prove that swearing can be a tremendous source of pain relief. When mixed with a bit humor, swearing actually jolts our brains into more expansive, tolerant and creative thinking spaces that make us much better problems solvers. This is especially handy when it comes to dealing with our bad bosses.

Having spent the past 10 years working in culture change and workplace behaviors in Australia and overseas, I'm endlessly curious about how to bring out the best in people – particularly at work. So, my friends and I decided to use all I'd learnt from my studies in positive psychology and neuroscience to fight back against our bad bosses and reclaim our sense of workplace happiness.

We wanted to learn when a bad situation was costing us too much, discover how to create miraculous outcomes in challenging circumstances, hold heavy conversations with a light touch and find the confidence and courage to act. In essence, to put some power back in the hands of employees, rid our lives of bad bosses, and make room for good bosses to flourish.

Supervisor abuse isn't always as blatant as a screaming temper tantrum; it can include taking personal anger out on us for no reason, rudely dismissing our ideas in a meeting, or simply being excessively critical of our work, while offering no constructive ways to improve it. The five reasons detailed in Chapters 4, 5, 6, 7 and 8 are based on all that science has so far learnt about how to build, protect and enjoy a level of well-being which allows us to flourish. In order to live our best lives, there are five essential elements which we should try to maximize: positive emotions, engagement, relationships, meaning and achievement (sometimes referred to as PERMA). When our bosses consistently and pervasively compromise any of these elements, we need to have the courage and the confidence to continue to cultivate and protect each of these elements.

Strangely, the more we used these techniques, the more often we found that there weren't that many truly bad bosses, but plenty of reasonable bosses doing a very bad job. For example, my boss wasn't a bad man by any stretch of the imagination. In fact, in the past he'd done many kind, encouraging and generous things to support my career. And, to his credit, when I clearly communicated my displeasure at his obsession with my resilience, he had the good grace to drop it and back off. His willingness to hear my feedback and immediately act on it makes him a good man with the potential to be a great boss. This certainty doesn't excuse his bad behavior, but it does offer hope that with knowledge, skills and awareness, better workplace outcomes can be created for us, our bosses and the organizations we work for, as detailed in Chapter 10.

You'll find our stories throughout this book (although names have been changed to protect the bad bosses).

Fortunately, for most of us, ours are not the stories of people who have been horrifyingly physically or psychologically abused that you occasionally come across. However, if you are being relentlessly bullied or harassed, sexually discriminated against, ripped off or have been unfairly terminated, you should seek legal advice immediately. And, at the back of the book, you'll find some guidance and resources which may assist.

I hope the honesty and courage of others helps you to find more success, joy, and fulfillment wherever your journey takes you.

Warmly,

Michelle

Section A:

How to overcome a bad boss

Chapter One

Do you have a bad boss problem?

If you're feeling hopeless, powerless, and traumatized due to a difficult boss – you're far from alone. Shocking research by renowned American psychologist Robert Hogan found that no matter whether a study was done in 1948, 1958, 1968, or 1998, in London, Baltimore, Seattle or Honolulu, among postal workers, milk truck drivers or school teachers, the results were pretty much identical – 75 per cent of the workforce reports that their immediate supervisor is the most stressful part of their job.[1]

This book is aimed at empowering you to turn around the difficulties posed by a bad boss. In the end, whether you decide to stay or quit, you'll learn a range of simple, practical skills that can make working for any kind of boss much better. You don't have to keep paying the high personal toll that workplace conflict brings. No matter what your role, you have the power to make your job much better.

This chapter is about our beliefs. The first step to overcoming a bad boss is to get real about what's actually happening and what we're telling ourselves. You don't have to do anything about it right now. Just be honest with yourself about what's really going down. When it comes to your bad boss, what exactly are you putting up with?

Case study 1

"Rachael, have you been under a lot of stress lately?" the doctor asked.

Rachael didn't know where to begin. Nine months ago, she started a new job at one of the country's most renowned colleges, working for a dean. The volume of work alone would have been enough to keep even the most capable employee on their toes, but coupled with this particular dean's tendency to withhold important pieces of information, Rachael found it impossible to feel like she was ever getting on top of things. Never one to let the opportunity to humiliate someone slip by, the dean seemed to take great delight in publicly reprimanding Rachael for every small detail which wasn't exactly right.

Having always taken great pride in the quality of her work, Rachael was horrified when the dean officially warned her about her poor performance. She started to hate her job, she also felt frustrated and helpless, no matter what she did she couldn't turn the dean around.

She couldn't believe that things had gotten so bad. And we, her friends – who didn't yet understand the healing power of telling our bosses to go fuck themselves – spent hours trying to work out how to help her. Happily, in the end, we were able to help Rachel put it right – but not before her entire life was put on the line.

What are you putting up with?

"My job has been incredibly difficult lately," Rachael acknowledged to the doctor.

When she'd first started her job, Rachael just assumed that the ranting, complaining, and unreasonable amounts of work were teething problems and once she figured out how the dean liked things done, everything would calm down. The dean was clearly a bit of a witch, but not wanting to appear overly sensitive, Rachael dismissed her behavior by reassuring herself that: "It's probably not that bad."

As the weeks rolled into months, however, Rachael learnt that not only did the dean behave this way with everyone, but that she was saving a special dose of scathing sarcasm and humiliation just for her. Apparently, all of her executive assistants had been given this special treatment so that they knew how easily they could be moved on. Slowly, but surely, Rachael's confidence and enthusiasm were being eroded, but calling out the dean on her behavior would require a mammoth effort on her part, so instead she soothed herself with the thought: "I'll just try and wait it out. I'm tough enough to take it."

When the seasons started to pass, the dean resorted to intimidating Rachael with threats about her job and vicious personal remarks. Having punished Rachael with an unfair end of year appraisal, the dean then decided to open an official file to detail Rachael's imagined incompetence. Ashamed that she'd put up with the dean's behavior for so long and fearful that there could be any truth to the accusations, Rachael finally hit the wall. She felt sick, tired and overwrought and resigned herself to the fact that: "There's nothing I can do about it, after all, she's the boss."

Like many of us, Rachael experienced that bad bosses have a tendency to creep up on us. Their offences usually start out quite small – a personal insult here, a dirty look there – making it easy to dismiss their unpleasant behavior. Unfortunately, while we're busy biting our tongue, a bad boss is testing out what they can get away with next by pushing the boundaries of frequency and effect. Left unchallenged they become increasingly brazen. Before we know it, we're under relentless attack and being twisted into knots of self-doubt, questioning if it's us or them that's the problem. Until eventually, like a battered spouse who has lingered too long, the situation feels impossible to turn around.

When it comes to bad bosses, little episodes gradually add up into big traumas. Instead of being honest with ourselves at the outset, we tend to dismiss the early warnings, hoping that it'll all blow over without us having to lift a finger. But bad bosses take this as a sign that we'll put up with whatever they can come up with until we find the confidence and courage to regain the power we have given them.

Initially, Rachael had hidden her head in the sand not wanting to have to confront the dean's behavior for fear of losing her well-paid job. But, as we're about to find out, ignoring a bad boss can leave us feeling completely stressed out.

Has your boss cast a spell of negativity?

"Doctor, why are you so worried about my stress levels?" Rachael asked.

An experienced, highly regarded executive assistant, Rachael had weathered her fair share of stressful roles and challenging bosses. From juggling the demands of complex diaries to dealing with desperate students and navigating academic politics, Rachael actually enjoyed mastering these challenges and it seemed like her best days were usually her busiest.

Lately, however, it seemed like the weight of stress in Rachael's job was pulling her down, down, down. She was grumpy and snappish, had more snide words than kind ones and nothing ever seemed to work out quite the way she planned. She was fed up, run-down and over everything. Spending time with Rachael was becoming increasingly exhausting.

Around this time, I was given an amazing opportunity to study with the founder of positive psychology, Professor Martin Seligman. As I flew the 21 hours from Australia to Philadelphia every three weeks to attend the University of Pennsylvania's Master of Applied Positive Psychology program, one of the first things this spritely, kind, wise and extraordinarily accomplished man taught me was that a little bit of stress in our lives can be a good thing.

While that felt instinctively right – I always seem to do a little better when under a bit of pressure – I was surprised to hear it coming from a man who is famous for building an empirical science around the study of what makes people happy. Always the scientist however, Marty is in no doubt that the evidence supports the facts that appropriate levels of negative emotions like sadness, anger and fear keep us grounded in reality and help us to flourish by motivating us to improve our experiences of life.[2]

Negative emotions, Marty taught me, served an important evolutionary purpose by flooding our brains whenever danger lurked nearby. In the blink of an eye, the stress caused by our bad feelings triggers an amazing set of bodily responses: our blood changes direction, moving from our brains to our arms and legs to get us moving; our adrenal glands release surges of adrenaline and cortisol to fire up our levels of energy; our interest in food and sex takes a back seat; endorphins are released to blunt any pain; and scores of neurotransmitters put our brains on high alert.[3]

When we were occasionally faced with the immediate threat of a saber-toothed tiger, this was an incredible feat of biology, which ensured we lived to tell the story. Millions of years later, this response still serves us well in the face of real danger or in small doses to propel us forward into learning experiences that we may fear.

The challenges of modern life, however – like putting up with bad bosses – means that our stresses aren't measured in moments anymore, but in hours, days, and sometimes even in months or years. Unfortunately, our bodies simply weren't built to handle consistently large amounts of stress and negativity.[4] Consequently, when the amount of stress we're experiencing starts to overwhelm us or lingers for too long, the buildup of negative emotions start to drag us down into the depths of helplessness, worthlessness and disgrace, compromising our ability to live the lives we want in almost every single way.[5] It turns out that the danger of negative feelings isn't in experiencing them – we all do –but in allowing them to rival our positive emotions in frequency and intensity.

Since I graduated, Marty has identified five elements that are essential to our well-being and our ability to flourish: positive emotions, engagement, relationships, meaning and accomplishment (or PERMA).[6] No one element ensures our well-being, but each contributes to it, so when a bad boss constantly makes our work miserable, tedious, lonely, senseless, or uninspiring, it creates negative emotions which when left to fester, cause us to languish.

Unchecked, the stress and negativity that's created by a bad boss can drain the very life out of us with dire consequences. Rachael knew that she'd been on edge, but she hadn't realized how stressful it had become to just walk into work each day or what this would eventually cost her.

If you're truly honest with yourself for a moment, just how much stress and negativity are being created by your bad boss?

What does your bad boss cost?

The diagnosis of cancer that followed, left Rachael shocked, but not surprised.

Shocked, because there was no family history of the disease and she'd always taken good care of her health. Not surprised, because she'd felt like something had been eating away at her insides these past few, horrible months.

The constant feelings of stress and negativity that resulted from the interactions with her boss had eroded Rachael's normal joy for life. Typically a keen runner, Rachael found that she was too tired to exercise. Usually a healthy eater, all she craved lately was sugar. Renowned for her deep sense of meaning for life, Rachael's faith had been almost completely extinguished. Ordinarily close to her family and friends, Rachael was avoiding them so that they couldn't see the mess she was in. Rarely ever sick a day in her life, Rachael now had cancer.

Could a bad boss cause all of that?

Negative emotions don't just make us feel bad, they quite literally change the way our brains and bodies operate. When we don't give ourselves the chance to rest and relax from a steady stream of negativity, it limits our ability to think and act.

An overload of negative emotions makes it difficult for us to perform well. They narrow our view of the world, making it hard to see opportunities. They also rob our brain of dopamine and serotonin – which are only stimulated by positive emotions – making it really tough to think quickly, creativity or laterally, leaving us in a decision-making rut. Left to linger, the stress of negative emotions eventually harms our ability to learn by shrinking our hippocampus, which is our fortress of memory. This is why studies show that the unhappiness inflicted by a bad boss decreases our effectiveness and undermines our performance, causing us to make less money, receive fewer promotions, and find our goals at work more difficult to achieve.[7]

By design, negativity inspires us to protect ourselves, which often means pulling back from others. Unfortunately, this separation can set us on a dark and lonely path that insulates us from the one thing we need most – the love and support of other people who care about us. So, it comes as no surprise that the tension caused by bad bosses has been found to detrimentally affect our marriages and families.[8]

Most frighteningly, when stress becomes chronic it eventually shifts our brain chemistry towards anxiety or depression and affects our immune response and cardiovascular functioning, elevating the risk of colds, diseases, strokes, and heart attacks. It's no coincidence that heart attacks are more likely to occur on Mondays or that employees who have a difficult relationship with their boss are 30 per cent more likely to suffer from coronary heart disease.[9]

The fact of the matter is that, people who experience an excess of cortisol get sick more often, recover slower and live shorter lives.[10] So, it's hard not to wonder, alongside her damaged career and exiled relationships, how else had the dean's behavior had impacted Rachel's health, given that various forms of cancer have now been associated with chronic and persistent negative images, expressed and embodied in feelings of helplessness and hopelessness.[11] What I discovered was that bad bosses shouldn't be taken lightly when it comes to their potential cost on our lives.

So, when it comes to the negativity and stress created by your bad boss, what is it costing you in terms of your career, your relationships, your health and your energy?

What story are you telling?

Rachael's doctor was clear; she needed to make big changes to her life.

"Look, there's still some debate about the role of chronic stress, like you've had in your job, and the development of cancer," the doctor explained. "But what we do know beyond doubt is that it doesn't help with the growth or spread of the disease. Rachael, in addition to surgery and treatment, we need to do all we can to minimize the stress and get you well again."

Rachael's first thought was to quit her job. As the doctor outlined her treatment plan however, she realized that she'd need all the paid sick leave she could get. So, exactly how was she meant to reduce her stress and negativity when she'd still be spending five days a week in the company of her very bad boss? The answer, and the outcome, surprised Rachael in both its simplicity and effectiveness.

Perhaps the very best secret Marty ever shared with me is that our emotions and behaviors are not triggered by events themselves, but by how we interpret what's happening to us. Narratives, or telling ourselves stories, are a natural response when we're trying to make sense of what's going on. Once a story is told, however, we have a tendency to take it as fact, which shapes our emotional responses and determines our ability to act.[12]

As I thought about the stories that Rachael had told about her boss, I suddenly understood how we'd helped to deprive her of a happy ending. When she'd first started working for the dean, to ease the shock of what she encountered, Rachael told us lots of "villain" stories about what a Crazy Old Witch (COW) her boss was. But when the dean started adding new forms of torture to her repertoire, Rachael's "victim" stories took off, she adopted the role of innocent bystander and started working all hours to try and prove she was just getting on with the job. By the time she was diagnosed with cancer, she had well and truly settled into her story of "helplessness" and accepted that she was completely powerless; after all, the dean was the boss.

Wanting to comfort our friend, as each story had been rolled out, we'd all vehemently agreed with the conclusions that Rachael had reached. We vilified the "villain" – declaring it was all the dean's fault. We despaired when Rachael was the innocent "victim," unlucky enough to end up with a bad boss. And we accepted that she was "helpless" when there seemed that nothing she could do would change the situation with her boss. Our intentions were good, but the results proved to be disastrous. Knowing what we know now, what we should have done was challenge her interpretations and where they were taking her.

Here's the kicker: sometimes the stories we tell are completely accurate – but not often. So, Marty challenged me to listen to the stories that I was creating. And, like a good detective, dispute the ones that weren't serving me well or swamping me with negativity by re-examining the facts.

I couldn't believe the difference this made to difficult experiences. Rather than wallowing in disappointment, anxiety, hopelessness, shame, or dread, it became possible to stall stress and negativity by getting curious about other ways to interpret the event. What set this situation off? Which negative thoughts and beliefs were triggered? How did those thoughts and beliefs make me feel? And how do those thoughts and beliefs compare to reality? What are the other facts of the situation? When I take in those facts – truly take them in – how do I feel?

Disputing negative thinking is scientifically proven to nip stress and negative emotions in the bud. [13] So; it's worth getting real with yourself and asking: what story are you telling about your bad boss? Do you lean towards being the "victim", working for the "villain" or feeling "helpless" most days?

Can you turn your story around?

There was undoubtedly a strong ring of truth in each of Rachael's stories. But by only focusing on all the things her boss did wrong, Rachael had created a downward spiral of stress, which led to more negative feelings about her boss and a vicious pattern of repetition. Rachael couldn't change the dean's behavior, but she could rescue herself by taking ownership of the stories she was telling.

That may sound simple enough, but remember, when our minds are in a dark and negative place, chemically, it's very difficult for our brains to think quickly, creativity or laterally which strands us in a decision-making rut. It's easier to challenge our stories if we first break the spiral of negative thinking with a small dose of positivity to reset our brains and help fuel our curiosity.[14]

Like a hidden reset button for our lives, Marty and his cohort of world-class researchers – many of whom you'll meet in the coming chapters – have built a compelling body of evidence that shows positive emotions flush out bad feelings thereby undoing their effects, quieting our hearts, calming our minds and quickly bringing our blood pressure and brain functioning back into line.[15] Studies show that two forms of positivity in particular – serenity and amusement – have been found to provide a swift antidote to physical stress and anxiety. In fact, just the anticipation of something funny has been found to reduce depression, anger, confusion, fatigue and tension.[16] It's what's known in my trade as the "undoing effect" of positivity.

The next time we caught up and Rachael started down her usual path of "helpless" bad boss stories, I listened for a while and then said: "Ah Rach, just tell her with the greatest respect to go fuck herself."

Now, if you were raised anything like Rachael and I, the idea of telling someone to go fuck themselves – even with the greatest respect – may seem unnecessarily crude or tasteless. However, studies show that provided we don't do it frequently, swearing can be a great source of pain relief.[17] I would never swear to intentionally harm another, but I have come to appreciate the value of telling someone who is causing me grief to respectfully go fuck themselves as a means of reclaiming some levity and serenity in stressful situations.

The very idea of Rachael telling this formidable woman to just go fuck herself painted a mental picture that kept us laughing for quite some time.

When we finally calmed down, I asked Rachael if there might be any other side to the story with her boss that would free her from the grip of helplessness. Using the techniques outlined in the next chapter, Rachael was able to eventually dispute many of the negative thoughts that she had about the dean. She didn't suppress them, push them aside or whitewash over them, but by finally seeing some of the other pieces of her reality she was literally able to dissolve her stress.

Although slightly disappointed that her moral righteousness had faded, the healthy dose of hopefulness that arrived in its place allowed Rachael to start focusing on what she wanted for herself and to let go of what she loathed about her boss. Gladly for all of us, Rachael has beaten her cancer to date by reducing the negativity in her life and heeding the care of some wonderful doctors. This, in turn, made her job more doable and eventually she was able to find a new role with a much nicer boss.

If the stories you're currently telling yourself about your bad boss have left you feeling helpless and spiraling down between negative thoughts and feelings – don't despair – just keep reading and I'll show you how I helped Rachael and others to turn it around. If the stories you're currently telling leave you feeling somewhat empowered, but you want some more tips on how to manage your bad boss, then you'll find plenty of ideas in the following pages as well.

In the meantime, a little dose of positivity makes us smarter and more motivated. So the next time negative emotions are unhelpfully darkening your life, see if you can find a reason to genuinely smile or laugh. Rachael and I still laugh at the idea of telling our bosses to go fuck themselves when they drive us up the wall.

Can you find a reason to smile – even if it's just briefly – and let some happy chemicals loose in your head to undo the spiral of negativity?

Questions to ask about what to do next

Every action we take is preceded by a question. Think about it. How did you come to be holding this book? You may have seen the cover and wondered what it was about, could it help you or would it be interesting to read? But before reading this book – no matter whether you bought it or it was given to you – you asked yourself some questions.

So, let me say it again because it bears repeating. Every action we take is preceded by a question. Unfortunately, most of the time we're completely unaware of the questions we've asked and how they are shaping the choices that we make.

To help raise your awareness about the power of questions in your life each chapter will have a "Questions to Ask" box at the end. Be sure to grab a pen and paper and reflect on your answers to these questions as you work out the best way to deal with your bad boss. These are only intended as thought starters, so as you get the hang of asking questions that open up possibilities, feel free to add more.

STEP 1: Get real about what you're telling yourself

1. When it comes to your bad boss, what are you honestly putting up with? Try to be specific about your boss' behavior – the what, when, and where.

2. If you're truly honest with yourself for a moment, just how much stress and negativity are being created by your bad boss?

3. What's this stress and negativity really costing you in terms of your career, your relationships, your health, and your energy?

4. What story are you telling about your bad boss? Do you lean towards being the "victim", working for the "villain" or feeling "helpless" most days?

5. Can you find a reason to smile – even if it's just briefly – and let some happy chemicals loose in your head to undo the spiral of negativity?

Chapter Two

Are you ready to act?

Gallup, one of the world's largest research organizations, has found that the person we least enjoy being around each day is our boss, with most us rating this time as worse than doing chores or even cleaning the house.[1] Another survey found that when it comes to improving our jobs more of us would prefer a new boss over a pay rise.[2] Perhaps this is because 60 per cent of workplace incivility is found to be top-down, with bosses subjecting us to inconsiderate words and deeds.[3] So why do we put up with it?

This chapter is about motivation: the second step to overcoming your bad boss is to own your own story so you're ready to act. By getting clear about what you want to fight for – rather than against – and recognizing your own beliefs, you can see if your own reactions are moving you towards the outcome you want. Then, by identifying your bosses' beliefs, you can learn how to avoid triggering off their bad behavior and stand up and take accountability for what you want and behave accordingly. What's going to motivate you to become the hero in your story?

Case study 2

"Amy, I'm heading out to visit some clients. I hope no one comes through with an axe while I'm out," chortled her boss. With that, she was gone in the company car, the car she refused to share with any of the staff.

Amy gritted her teeth and waited until she heard the door slam. "Bitch," muttered Amy.

Amy had recently returned from visiting one of the center's rehabilitation clients to find their office unlocked and unattended. Some of the people they dealt with at the center faced considerable mental health challenges so it was part of the small team's Health and Safety Policies that, as counselors, they shouldn't be there alone with clients. Unfortunately, with no one manning the office and everything left open Amy had no way to know if she'd find somebody waiting for her. Rather than put herself at risk, Amy called the police who asked her to wait for them to check everything was safe before entering.

When her boss returned and discovered that the police had been called, she went deathly silent, marched into her office and slammed the door. When Amy knocked later to raise her concerns about office safety, her boss pursed her lips and asked, "Will that be all?" Then, she pointed Amy to the door.

Rather than following up the issue with Amy in the following days, her boss started cracking jokes like the one about the axe and encouraged the rest of the staff to make jokes at Amy's expense. What was wrong with Amy's boss? And how was she meant to deal with her?

Do you know where you're going?

On reflection, Amy realized that she shouldn't have been surprised. During the past 18 months since joining the center, she'd seen her boss flagrantly ignore policies whenever it suited her. Six months ago, her boss had somehow gotten herself promoted by the board, which included access to a company car to be shared with staff. Not only were none of them allowed to use the car, even though it sat in the car park most days, but Amy's boss seemed to think nothing of using the company's gas allowance to ferry her children around on holidays.

Amy really liked her clients and it gave her a great sense of satisfaction to be part of their recovery, but her boss' flagrant abuses of non-profit resources and disregard for her staff was making it increasingly difficult for her to enjoy her work. Since the relentless jokes about "safety" had started, she found herself dreading going to work and doing all she could to avoid her boss. Well aware of how the costs of negativity can add up, Amy knew that she had to find a way to make the situation stop.

By the time she sat down and shared what was really happening with me, Amy had christened her supervisor the "bitch boss" as her feelings of helplessness and bitterness threatened to overwhelm her. "Ah Amy," I said after her story of anxiety and frustration came pouring out, "just tell her to go fuck herself."

This gave us a good laugh as we imagined how the "bitch boss" would take such a suggestion – maybe she'd find that some jokes aren't as funny as they seem! And it created a space for me to ask Amy two important questions, which could turn her story around.

First, I asked: "If you could wake up tomorrow and head into work to find that a miracle had occurred overnight, what would be different? Really think about it Amy. What would you be doing? How would your boss be behaving? What would it feel it like?"

When Amy imagined her miracle, she was still working in her job, but was being treated as a valued member of the team. She felt safe to go to work because her colleagues took care of each other. She was appreciated for her counseling experience, ideas and efforts. Resources were fairly shared and policies followed. And she had a relationship with her boss that was built on respect.

Positive future images weave a powerful magic through our stories. Just the very idea of having the rewards that come from getting what we want is enough to kick start a cascade of dopamine through key neural pathways in our brain that have the power to move us from intention into action.[4] This is why positive images have been found to pull us forward into new possibilities that fuel us with hope, put us on the road to finding solutions and help us to realize that we have the power to make things happen.[5]

For example, only when English athlete Roger Bannister dared to imagine that a mile could be run in less than four minutes did he accomplish this previously declared "impossible" feat. And medical "miracles" of physiological repair are experienced by up to two-thirds of participants in medical placebo tests because they are led to believe that they are receiving a revolutionary drug, rather than a simple sugar pill.[6]

Now that she felt a glimmer of hope, I asked Amy the second question, which I knew she was going to find much harder: "Amy, when it comes to your boss, have you been behaving as though this is what you want? Are you one hundred per cent the innocent victim in this story, or are there things that you may have unintentionally been doing that are keeping you from the miracle you want?"

Amy went very quiet. I could tell by the look on her face that this wasn't a question she liked. Eventually, with some reluctance, Amy acknowledged that although it was her boss who was the one breaking all the policies, there might have been some things that Amy had also done which hadn't really helped.

Perhaps she'd been so busy painting her boss as the "villain" and calling her names that Amy hadn't been as friendly or warm as she usually was. Maybe she'd been so busy shaking her head as the "victim" of her boss' abuses that she hadn't tried to address ways that resources, like the car, could be shared more fairly. And it was conceivable that Amy had been so immersed in feeling "helpless" about her lack of safety at work that she had embarrassed her boss in the way that she had dealt with it by calling the police.

Unfortunately, when we believe that nothing we do counts and external forces – like our bad boss – dictate how events unfold, it's hard to avoid falling into the insidious grip of learned helplessness. Before long, we stop trying and simply give up.

Finding that our actions are having a direct effect on some outcomes, however – even if they're not the ones we consciously intended or feel particularly proud of – helps us to see that we're not completely powerless and allows us to feel more in control of our lives. As a result, our stress levels drop, our motivation rises and we're more likely to act in ways that lead to the results we want.[7]

I didn't want to hurt Amy or make her mad, but I had learnt by now that there's never only one side to a story that involves two people. I wanted to shake Amy out of her story of helplessness and into her "heroes" story so that she could find a way to rescue herself from her bad boss.

The first step was to help her realize what she was fighting for – her miracle – rather than fighting against her boss. After all, every hero needs a good cause.

The second step was to help Amy see that she wasn't powerless because her behaviors were having plenty of impact (she'd distanced herself from her boss by calling her names, she'd inadvertently encouraged misuse of service resources and she'd embarrassed her boss about issues of safety around the office) but were moving her away from the things she wanted. She was going to need a new plan to make her miracle happen.

There is incredible power in realizing that our behavior matters because for anything to change, someone has to start acting differently.[8] Heroes stand tall and take accountability for what they want and act accordingly.

If you could wake up tomorrow and head into work to find that a miracle occurred overnight what would be different? When it comes to the relationship with your boss, have you been behaving as though this is the miracle you want?

What beliefs are driving your reactions?

Everyone agreed that Amy's boss was a pretty selfish person. Not only did she hoard resources, like promotions and office cars, she also had a tendency to bend the rules to suit herself, but refused to bend them for others. For example, she left the office at 4pm every day even though she was meant to be there for another hour, but refused to allow anyone else to finish early even if their work was all done. She also brought her dog to work every day, but refused to allow other staff members to have any of their pets visit the office. So far, Amy hadn't found a policy that her boss wasn't prepared to break if she could get away with it.

Amy had worked with difficult people before – loads of them – but something about her boss got under her skin and brought out the worst in her. If Amy was going to start behaving more positively, she needed to find a way to stop her boss' bad behavior from constantly setting her off.

During my studies, I was lucky enough to be taught the skills of resilience by the amazing Karen Reivich. A bundle of energy, curiosity, and creativity, Karen trains leaders around the world, from businesses to schools to the US Army, in how to bring out the best in themselves and other people.

For years, I'd been aware that in situations where I felt anxious or stressed there was a little voice whispering away inside of my head, "I knew you weren't really good enough" and "Now everyone will find out". Every time these thoughts would fire off, I'd want to hide from the world in shame and often ended up walking away from people and situations that stressed me out.

Karen taught me that we all have these types of "ticker-tape beliefs" running in our heads. They shape the way we feel and behave when our anxieties are triggered off by trying to explain why things are happening and what will happen next. Best of all, she showed me how to get hold of these beliefs in the midst of adversities, challenges or new experiences and control the way they made me feel so that I could act in a manner that was productive and appropriate to the facts, rather than being led by knee-jerk responses.

This technique is part of cognitive behavior therapy. It teaches us to watch for the Adversities (A) that trigger off stress and negative emotions, like when Amy's boss abused the office policies. Then, to look for the most common Consequences (C) of these situations in the terms of the behaviors that we exhibit, like Amy feeling overcome with anger and swearing about her boss. It shows us how to identify the Belief (B) most commonly associated with these actions, like the feeling that Amy's boss is violating her right to be treated fairly. And then teaches us to Dispute (D) its accuracy by challenging the belief or thinking of other reasons.[9]

While most of us grow up believing that the world operates A– C, we experience an Adversity and our behavior is the Consequence, this is simply not the case. Instead, what actually happens is A – B – C, we experience an Adversity, our Beliefs about the event kick in, and then the Consequences of feelings and behaviors follow. When we learn to Dispute these beliefs by looking for specific evidence, we can free ourselves of the negative emotions they create and move forward more positively.[10]

Given everyone's Beliefs are associated with their own set of language, some common patterns have proven universal in their Consequences and this has been well-researched and documented. I've found this chart that Karen gave me a handy guide to follow:

Beliefs	Consequences
Something bad may happen	Anxiety, fear
Sense of loss	Sadness, depression
Not good enough	Embarrassment, withdrawal
Violation of own rights	Anger, wrath
Violation of another's rights	Guilt

By looking for the patterns that most frequently brought Amy unstuck when dealing with her boss, she was able to see that the Belief that her boss was somehow violating her rights was the one that set her off into spirals of negativity. When she was able to Dispute this Belief with plausible alternatives – maybe Amy's boss went home early to care for her children and logged on later to make up the extra time rather than short-changing her employer and colleagues – Amy's anger dissipated and she was able to respond in a much calmer and more respectful manner.

The good news is that this technique proves that we have more control over how we feel than most of us think. Learning how to regulate our emotions and control our impulses by challenging our Beliefs frees us to act with empathy, optimism and confidence.[11] What are the common Adversities that trigger your worst Consequences when it comes to your boss? Which Beliefs are linked with these behaviors? Could there be any other alternative explanations?

What beliefs are driving your boss?

There was no doubt that Amy's boss behaved quite appallingly at times. Each month, the staff had to prepare an update on their work and any issues they were facing for the board. Amy's boss was meant to gather the reports and forward them on, but lately had taken to editing them by taking credit for successful projects and deleting any complaints raised by the team. It was no wonder she'd been promoted. How could a person behave so atrociously?

Now that Amy knew what she wanted, believed she wasn't completely powerless and understood how to regulate her responses. The next step was to get her to understand what was driving her boss so that she could hatch a clever plan and make her miracle happen. Amy understood intuitively that when it came to her boss it was all about her boss and nobody else, but she wasn't sure how to manage around this fixation so that she could create the outcome that she longed for.

Karen taught me the technique of cognitive behavior therapy to use for myself or when coaching clients to move through their challenges. Personally, I've also found it an amazingly powerful way to understand and disarm difficult people – like a bad boss. For example, while bad bosses come in all shapes and sizes, there are some common patterns, which have been observed to their beliefs and behaviors. For me, it updates Karen's table as follows:

Boss Type	Beliefs	Consequences
Authoritarian Boss "My way or the highway"	Something bad may happen	Anxiety and fear
Laissez-Faire Boss Does as little as possible	A sense of loss	Sadness and depression
Narcissistic Boss "Me, me, me, me, mine"	Not good enough	Embarrassment and withdrawal
Bullying Boss "You are worthless"	Violation of own rights	Anger and wrath
Mixed Bag Boss Never know where you stand	Violation of another's rights	Guilt

Amy's boss was a classic "Narcissistic Boss" who encounters an Adversity (A) and withdraws in embarrassment (C). This is most likely due to their fear that they are not really good enough – especially when compared to others (B). This is the type of personality that's perfectly embodied by the character of Michael Scott in The Office. Michael means well (most of the time), but his self-centered and cowardly ways always get in the way of him managing his employees well. This type of boss takes credit for our work and hoards the resources and rewards for themselves to make up for what they fear they lack. Worried about not really being good enough, they try to cover this up by making it all about them – all of the time.[12]

There's also the "Laissez-Faire Boss" who encounters an Adversity (A) and simply goes missing or withdraws from decisions because they feel sad, down, dejected, or depressed (C). This is most likely due to the fear of loss of something real – like a relationship or job – or intangible, like self-worth (B). A close friend once had a boss like this, who – afraid of losing their good working relationship – would suddenly disappear into thin air whenever a difficult decision arose. Calls were not returned, emails went unanswered and meetings were suddenly cancelled until the deadline passed and the opportunity with it. Afraid of loss, this type of boss ends up making us do all the work so that they have nothing on the line.[13]

In contrast, when the "Authoritarian Boss" encounters an Adversity (A) they become incredibly anxious and start trying to control or micromanage everything

(C). They most likely believe that something bad is about to happen that they'll be incapable of managing (B). Meryl Streep's fabulous portrayal of Miranda Priestly, the boss of a fashion magazine, is a great example of this type of boss in action. She is rude, direct, task-orientated, picky and demanding. In an effort to tame their anxiety, this boss is likely to declare that, "it's my way or the highway".[14]

Meanwhile, when the "Bullying Boss" encounters an Adversity (A) they start showing annoyance, irritability, acrimony, outrage, fury, and wrath (C). They are most likely to fear that someone has set out to deliberately harm them by treating them unfairly or thwarting their success (B). This is why my boss would suddenly start yelling or plotting vengeance whenever he thought people were screwing up his chances of success. This type of boss fears being harmed or violated so strikes by tearing us down to size. [15]

And, of course, there is the "Mixed Bag Boss" who when encountering an Adversity (A) goes out of their way to make amends (C) out of fear that they've mistreated you in some way (B). This is the type of boss who one day gives you the cold shoulder and the next day is trying to be your best friend. Whenever this boss feels guilty for having been inconsiderate, unkind, or worse, they have a tendency to overcorrect, making their moods and actions completely unpredictable from one day to the next. This is also the type of boss with whom we never know where we stand.[16]

Most bosses have a bias that leans to one particular style, but this is not always the case. Some bosses will have two or more "ticker-tape beliefs", which regularly appear in response to Adversities. It's important not to jump to conclusions, but instead pay careful attention to what we're really consistently seeing.

One more word of caution; sometimes when the Consequences seem out of proportion to the paired Belief this is a sign that an "underlying, iceberg belief"– rather than a "ticker-tape belief" – has been struck. Underlying beliefs tend to be general propositions or rules for living – values about how the world ought to be and how we should operate within it. They're often based around our ideas about achievement, acceptance and control and to get to the bottom of them we may need to put our heads in the lion's mouth and ask our bosses: What's upsetting you most about the situation? What's the worst part about that for you? What does that say about you? What's so bad about that? You'll know you've hit the belief when you – and possibly your boss – suddenly hit the "aha moment" and everything makes sense. [17]

When Amy was able to see that her boss' embarrassment of not being good enough was what was driving her bad behavior, rather than a deliberate intention to harm her, a huge sense of relief descended. Looking at what had been happening through this lens allowed Amy to feel just a tiny glimpse of empathy and compassion for the flawed human being that her boss clearly was. Imagine getting to be the boss and then spending all your time worrying that someone would work out that you weren't really good enough!

Don't get me wrong, our intention here is not to excuse bad bosses. But as annoying as it may be to believe that there is anything rational behind their behavior, it is essential that we consider what is making them act so unreasonably to reach the happy ending we desire.

The reality is that we are born as sense-making machines who want to predict, understand and control what happens around us, so when we can interpret beliefs, behaviors and consequences in ways that add up, we move past the feelings of disquieting uncertainty and feel safe, intelligent and confident again.[18] It boosts our levels of positivity and prepares us to act.

Although Amy still didn't like her boss' selfish attitude and bad behaviors, identifying her boss' Beliefs took the personal sting out of the situation. In addition, it disarmed her boss' ability to get under Amy's skin so that she could put her energy into creating the miracle she wanted.

So, is there a Belief on the chart above that can help you make sense of your bad boss' behavior? If the Beliefs don't match the "type" of boss I've suggested above, don't get hung up on this, just pay particular attention to connecting the Beliefs and Consequences.

A bad person or just bad at their job?

Unfortunately, there is a very small group of bosses, about five out of every 100, who may be suffering from a psychological disorder that causes long-lasting, uncontrollable emotional disregulation. People who are diagnosed as psychopaths or borderline personalities – to name just a few of the disorders – suffer from inflexible and pervasive patterns of thinking, which impairs their abilities and causes them serious problems. The symptoms of each disorder varies, but the common element appears to be the diminished ability to empathize with others – to feel what another person is feeling – which enables them to perpetrate their acts of cruelty.[19]

The biggest challenge with these disorders is that often the boss involved has not been diagnosed. Unaware of the neurological and psychological challenges they're facing, they receive no support or medication (if appropriate) to manage their thought patterns. While many of these disorders are permanent and incurable, most can also now be managed with varying degrees of success provided your boss is aware that they have a neurological condition they need to monitor.

Having lived with a dear friend before he was diagnosed with bipolar disorder, I can tell you that working with an undiagnosed boss would be a very trying experience. It's impossible to make sense of the behaviors of people with these illnesses unless the diagnosis is pin-pointed.

If you suspect that your boss is significantly low in empathy and high in erratic behaviors and this is negatively impacting your life, then it's either time to look for another job, or have a serious discussion with your boss' supervisor. If you choose the latter, be sure to have kept a diary of what is happening – dates, times, triggers and consequences – and try to bear in mind that for all the pain they've caused, this is potentially a person in real need of medical or psychological help.

Happily, for most of us (Amy included), it's easier to make sense of a bad boss' behavior. For example, if Amy's boss had a ticker-tape of beliefs running through her head that said, "I'm not really good enough", then perhaps she thought that belittling Amy would take people's mind off the fact that she, her boss, had violated the workplace safety policy. It didn't make it right, but it did reframe the decision to be grounded on her boss' unfounded fears rather than an assumption of Amy's neuroticism.

Although this now made complete sense to Amy, she couldn't help but wonder if anything else was going on for her boss. One colleague who had worked with the woman prior to this role vowed that she wasn't that bad and could be fun and kind-hearted, yet Amy found her to be mean and selfish. It was as though when she was promoted she'd added a dollop of power craziness to her bubbling fear that she wasn't really good enough.

On top of her sudden delusions of grandeur, the pressure to quickly deliver results seemed to heightening Amy's boss' anxiety to lunatic levels. Her obsession with speed meant she cut corners left, right, and center and then blamed the team when issues appeared. Intent on proving that she was a management superstar to the board, Amy's boss then bullied the team to cover it up.

Clearly struggling, the woman had then gone and sought a mentor from the board to guide her. Initially, the team had breathed a sigh of relief, thinking help was at hand, but it turned out that the new mentor was even crankier and nastier than Amy's boss. Rather than calming Amy's boss down, the mentor seemed to infect a new level of haughtiness into her boss' antics.

This further disheartened Amy because study after study has shown that when people are given power over us it can do funny things to their heads – from making them more willing to electrocute a stranger with a heart condition[20] to physically abusing a volunteer "prisoner" while playing the role of a volunteer "prison guard".[21] When people (regardless of personality) wield power, research demonstrates that they become more focused on themselves, less focused on others and start to believe that they are above the rules that apply to everyone else.[22]

Unfortunately, today many organizations compound the problems of power by relying on fear and pressure to motivate our bosses to improve team performance. The promises of recognition and rewards and the threats of blame and punishments – coupled with unrelenting time pressures – creates a melting pot of mental neurosis capable of turning even the nicest person into the most horrible boss., [23]

Our emotions are highly contagious, so when our boss is behaving like a wounded bear their negativity starts to spread to everyone around them. This is because the amygdala in our brain can read and identify an emotion in another person's face within 33 milliseconds and then just as quickly prime us to feel the same. Couple this with our mirror neurons – specialized brain cells that can actually sense and then mimic the feelings, actions and physical sensations of another person – and it's no wonder our bad boss' negative emotions can start to seep into us, whether we like it or not.[24]

Apparently, being the boss is not always an easy job. This doesn't excuse their bad behavior, but by temporarily turning down the volume on our own priorities and experiences and choosing to hear our bosses with a certain measure of kindness, we're able to tap into the feeling of empathy which allows us to create bridges across unresolvable conflicts.[25]

Empathy forms a space for us to respect our differences, even if the problems themselves cannot be solved. By understanding her boss' "not good enough" beliefs and appreciating the pressures of her job, Amy was able to find a tiny flicker of empathy and compassion for her boss. It also helped to humanize her boss and for Amy to accept that she was just another person who was probably trying to do her best.

Personally, I believe that there are very few genuinely bad bosses, but rather an abundance of bosses who are bad at their jobs. Most bosses don't want to leave people feeling demeaned, disrespected, and de-energized – as we'll discuss later, it's a terrible way to run a business. Yet most bosses are also never offered the knowledge, skills or experiences they require to succeed in their job. This certainty doesn't excuse their horrible behavior, but it does offer us hope that by understanding what drives our bad bosses we can more positively impact our future.

Amy still despised the way her boss was treating her, but as the days went on, she found that most of the time it no longer made her feel as though her rights were being violated. Many of the choices her boss made still seemed ludicrous, but being able to make sense of them more quickly ensured that they sent Amy into less of an emotional tailspin. Amy also became much better at couching her requests in a way that wouldn't embarrass her boss or make her feel not good enough. And slowly, little by little, things calmed down enough with her bad boss so that Amy was confident enough to find a new job in a much nicer and safer workplace that still helped others.

No matter where you find yourself currently with your bad boss, it's always possible to become the hero in your own story and rescue yourself. Heroes fight for a cause, they know what they want and they behave accordingly. In addition, heroes learn how to manage their responses so that their beliefs don't ignite fears that will trigger knee-jerk responses.

What's more, heroes also take the time to understand the fear-based beliefs of people who are behaving badly so that they can disarm them of their ability to inflict personal injury. And heroes know that empathy is the most powerful weapon in unresolvable conflicts because it frees their attention from focusing on what's wrong to finding ways to build on what's right. In the next chapter, I'll show you how to use this liberation to get the outcomes that you want.

Someone once asked me in the middle of a fight: "Is it more important at this moment for you to be right or to be happy?" It was a good question, which immediately caused me to pause and then change direction. In the end, being right when it comes to our bad boss doesn't count for much when it leaves you experiencing a world of pain.

Being able to be happy at work on the other hand – even if no one else acknowledges that you were right – increases our effectiveness and fuels our performance. This, in turn, enables us to make more money, achieve goals more easily, receive more promotions, enjoy better job security, receive better supervisor ratings and avoid becoming burnt-out, thereby providing the best revenge. [26]

By understanding their beliefs and the pressures of their job are you able to find a flicker of empathy for your boss?

Questions to ask about what to do next

Grab a pen and paper and reflect on your answers to these questions as you work out how you can be the hero of your own story. These are only intended as thought starters, so as you get the hang of asking questions that open up possibilities, feel free to add more.

STEP 2: Own your own story so that you're ready to act

1. Heroes stand up and take accountability for what they want and act accordingly. If you could wake up tomorrow and head into work to find that a miracle occurred overnight, what would be different? When it comes to the relationship with your boss, have you been behaving as though your miracle can and will happen?

2. Learning how to regulate our emotions and control our impulses by challenging our Beliefs frees us to act with empathy, optimism and confidence. What are the common Adversities that trigger your worst Consequences when it comes to your boss? Which Beliefs are linked with these behaviors? Could there be any other alternative explanations?

3. Is there a Belief on the chart below which can help you make sense of your bad boss' behavior? If the Beliefs don't match the "type" of boss I've suggested above, don't get hung up on this, just pay particular attention to connecting the Beliefs and Consequences, which have been well-proven.

Boss Type	Beliefs	Consequences
Authoritarian Boss "My way or the highway"	Something bad may happen	Anxiety and fear
Laissez-Faire Boss Does as little as possible	A sense of loss	Sadness and depression
Narcissistic Boss "Me, me, me, me, mine"	Not good enough	Embarrassment and withdrawal
Bullying Boss "You are worthless"	Violation of own rights	Anger and wrath
Mixed Bag Boss Never know where you stand	Violation of another's rights	Guilt

4. Empathy allows a space for us to respect our differences, even if the problems themselves cannot be solved. By understanding their beliefs and the pressures of their job are you able to find a flicker of empathy for your boss?

Chapter Three

Can you get the outcome you want?

Unfortunately, the numbers don't lie; most of us are likely to encounter a bad boss at some stage in our lives. And when it does happen to us, the feeling of shame can be overwhelming. What's more, our tendency to want to hide behind secrecy and silence, so that people who care about us don't know what is happening, is one of the ways in which bad bosses become so potent in our lives.

This chapter examines the importance of connecting with someone else – telling someone you trust what's really happening and how you're feeling about that. And then, the next step is joining forces with this person to help you to think through ways to achieve a positive, win-win outcome with your boss.

Case study 3

"Tim, you're going to be gone for eight weeks. The only way we can cover the gap in your sales numbers while you're away is for you to make them up before you leave," explained his boss. "It's that or no honeymoon, sorry."

Tim had only been with the bank for a couple of months and had really been enjoying his role – up until this moment. He sold financial insurance to wealthy individuals to protect them when hard times took hold. Although Tim was still learning the ropes, his results to date had been great. But now this! It was less than a month until Tim's wedding. There was no way he'd find enough buyers before he left.

Unable to bear the idea of letting his fiancé down, Tim started arriving at work at 7am and staying until well past 10pm each night. He combed his client lists, following up every contact who hadn't already purchased from him. He charmed, he cajoled and he begged to try and get the bottom line signed. But it just wasn't going to be enough.

Then, each day, around noon, Tim's boss would walk by his desk and ask: "How are those numbers looking? Remember, there's no honeymoon if those sales numbers aren't in." It was just the type of encouragement Tim needed least.

If that wasn't bad enough, after a steady diet of takeaway foods and no exercise, Tim's wedding suit was feeling very tight. He'd had to cancel his buck's party and tell his best man that he simply didn't have the time. And, that morning he'd yelled at his future bride as she tried to finalize their plans. Eventually, she'd demanded to know what was up and the whole sorry saga came out. Realizing that he needed help, she called me on the phone and then Tim and I had a very long chat.

Why is it worth reaching out?

I knew that Tim didn't really want to talk about what was happening; he had only called me because his fiancé made him. Knowing that he needed help though, I kept prodding him with gentle questions until his story of misery, frustration, and despair spilled out.

It was only a week before the wedding and Tim felt like a complete mess. He'd been pressuring and pleading with virtual strangers to buy his policies – proven tactics for losing a sale and permanently damaging your relationships. He was snapping at other team members to get him more data and speed up the reports so his deals could be closed. But there just weren't enough hours in the day or buyers in the market to get his target met. Tim felt like his head was going to explode and was ashamed and embarrassed that his boss had him running around chasing his own tail. In short, Tim's mojo was completely trashed.

One of my all-time heroes is wholeheartedness researcher Brene Brown. Brene's work started with hundreds of interviews with people to uncover how shame and fear impact our lives. She then examined how we can avoid those negative emotions sneaking up and stealing our sense of worthiness and driving us into a spiral of negativity, which makes it difficult to step up and own our own stories.

What Brene has discovered though, is that shame can't survive being shared with another. By bringing our shame out into the light and reaching out to someone we trust to talk about what is happening, we increase our power and potential to put the situation right[1] and overcome our bad boss.

44

When Tim's story was told I simply said: "You know what Tim, I think that you should tell your boss with the greatest respect to take his extra sales numbers and go fuck himself." You won't be surprised by now to hear that the sheer relief at imagining he could simply tell his boss to go fuck himself gave Tim and I a good laugh. And the more I insisted he should just tell his boss to go fuck himself the more we laughed. For the first time in a month, a much needed dose of positivity crept into Tim's life.

When I'd tried this line on Rachael I knew that occasional swearing was a way to relieve pain and move her brain into a more positive space, but I hadn't fully appreciated the power that comes from laughing together. When playing with Brene's work, however, I came to understand that when we share this kind of knowing laughter with someone else, we experience a sense of relief and connection by disclosing our shame and realizing that we're not alone. Without another word being spoken, it allows us to say to one another, "I'm with you. I get it," and breaks the sinister grip of isolation.[2]

When this happens, the feeling of relief is immediate. Suddenly, our shame becomes something manageable again. It moves us away from thoughts like, "I'm so stupid for allowing this to happen," to "this situation is ridiculous, I'm sure there's a better way to achieve this outcome". In one brief moment, it allows us to realize that it's okay to be vulnerable.

So, how can something as simple as laughing together undo our knots of shame? It just so happens that other people are both an antidote for depression and a prescription for high performance, because they can inject positivity – like amusement – into the direst situations.[3]

If the shame of a bad boss has silenced you, it's time to reach out to someone you can trust and share your story. Who can provide the safety, empathy, and support required for you to tell them about both sides of the story – the victim and the hero – that you are experiencing with your boss?

How are two heads better than one?

Tim wanted to keep his job and be able to go on his honeymoon without feeling guilty about the team's numbers. He also didn't want his job to overshadow the joy of his wedding. And he definitely didn't fancy a relationship with his boss in which unreasonable and unrealistic demands were the standard mode of operation. But when pushed, Tim also reluctantly admitted that he hadn't spent the past month behaving as though this was the outcome he was working toward. In fact, it turned out that chaining himself to his desk days before his wedding to reach an impossible sales target didn't come close to the miracle he was envisioning.

Tim went on to offer excuse after excuse – all of them reasonable – about why he couldn't do anything differently. But I'm a firm believer that behind every excuse lays a fear that's holding us back and sure enough, when we dug down into it, Tim had a "ticker-tape belief" that something bad may happen; in this case that if he didn't make his numbers he'd be fired. On reflection, Tim realized that this was not something his boss had ever threatened, but may have come from his parents' warnings that anyone who takes an eight week honeymoon is likely to lose their job.

The problem with unfounded fears is that, as we saw earlier, they cloud our brains with negative emotions making it difficult for us to think expansively, creatively and collaboratively, which are exactly the things we need most to hatch a clever plan and overcome a bad boss. This is why in the midst of challenges and stress at work, nothing is more crucial to our success than holding on to good people around us.[4]

This may sound simple enough, but remember, during these periods when shame often besets us, our most natural response is to retreat into our shells, leaving us feeling miserable, dejected, overwhelmed and all alone. But it's precisely at these moments that instead of divesting, we need to invest in our relationships. When we reach out to other people we can count on we instantaneously multiple our emotional, intellectual, and physical resources. It's one of the reasons that most breakthroughs are created in collaborative circles than by people working alone.[5]

As we continued to talk, I was able to use my more positive brain to lead Tim's brain out of the fear, stress, and negativity, which was making it impossible for him to see opportunities to deal with his boss. I did this by asking questions because I knew that when we start to seek out novel or uncertain information, our curiosity fires up our feel-good levels of dopamine. As we worked through the questions outlined earlier, Tim came to understand that he shared with his boss the "ticker tape belief" that "something bad may happen".

Tim remembered that the team's revenues were down as a whole and his boss was under the pump to get these numbers up. Although Tim was reasonably new, he'd been one of the star closers for the team, so it was feasible that his boss' sudden authoritarian hysteria was an effort to squeeze out more sales before Tim went on his honeymoon. Unfortunately, because of Tim's own "ticker tape belief" that "something bad may happen" he'd taken this extra pressure to mean his job was on the line, although his boss had never indicated that this was a possibility.

As Tim's "aha moment" kicked in, a calm quietness settled over him like a storm that had suddenly passed. "What on earth have I been doing?" he asked, suddenly laughing with relief as he started to realize how these beliefs had driven his behaviors. "More importantly what should I be doing instead?"

When our head is a jumble of negativity, we lack the necessary chemicals in our brain to think at our best. This is why it's essential that we reach out to someone else and bolster our own resources. Not only do we benefit from their clearer heads, but each time we make a positive social connection, the pleasure-inducing hormone oxytocin is released into our bloodstream, immediately reducing anxiety and improving our ability to concentrate and focus as levels of cortisol come down. [6]

Our relationships with others are our best guarantee of lowering our stress and raising our well-being.[7] Excited now by the possibilities of finding a better way to manage his boss, Tim suddenly wanted to talk and talk and talk. Who can help you double your resources by providing a positive, optimistic and innovative brain that you can bounce ideas off?

Do you know how to fall up?

Although Tim deplored the tactics that his boss was using, he was starting to understand why he was behaving so unreasonably. But the approach the guy was taking was never going to work – it smacked of desperation. So, Tim couldn't help, but feel a small flicker of empathy for his boss. There had to be a better way to get the outcomes they both wanted.

Luckily, since the dawn of time our brains have constantly created and revised mental maps to help us navigate our way through life. Mapping things like our physical environment, strategies for getting food and shelter and the possible effects of our actions comes as second nature. So, when we're faced with a crisis or adversity, there are always three mental paths available to us.

There's the first path, which keeps us circling around in the place we're already at so the negative event makes no real difference to us. Next, there's the second path, which leads us down towards more negative consequences leaving us far worse off than when we started. And then there's the third path, which leads us from failure or setback to a place of learning and growth so that we're even stronger and more capable than before we fell. [8]

Ironically, in a crisis we tend to form incomplete mental maps and when struck by fear and helplessness, we don't even bother looking for the third path. This is why we need to hang on to more positive-thinking friends who can help us explore the most productive path to rising above our bad boss.

Knowing now that if he didn't change the way he was dealing with his boss, the pressure of being micromanaged would continue every time their numbers became difficult, Tim decided that he needed to find a path, which would lead him up and beyond the current crisis to create the type of long-term relationship he wanted with his boss.

So, tapping his curiosity once more, I challenged Tim to suspend all judgments for the next two minutes and try to generate at least six endings to the following sentence: "To improve my job and my current relationship with my boss by five per cent I could..."

Here's what he came up with:

- Try to ignore my boss' anxiety, keep boosting my own positivity and hope for the best.

- Take my boss for a drink and let him get it all off his chest to ease his anxiety.

- Tell my boss that the sales target simply can't be reached and he should prepare for the consequences.

- Ask my fellow team members to join me in appealing to our boss to chill out because we're all doing our best.

- Talk to my boss and see if we can come up with alternative ways to deal with the sales pressure during my leave period.

- Tell my boss that with the greatest respect, when it comes to his unreasonable expectations of magic sales numbers, he can go fuck himself, but that I'd be happy to help him make it up in eight weeks when I'm back.

By emptying our minds of expectations about what will happen next or what's "supposed" to happen, this technique – known as sentence stem completion – allows us to tap into the hidden knowledge we all have but are often unaware of.[9]

Given the miracle you want and the understanding of what's driving your boss, how would you complete the sentence: "To improve my job and my current relationship with my boss by five per cent I could ..."? Remember, two heads are better than one so don't be afraid to ask for some help and suspend your logical thinking for a bit. If you get stuck, it helps to repeat this exercise each day for up to a week before you evaluate what you've got.

Is it really necessary to say "fuck"?

When he was done, I asked Tim to go over the responses and identify the ones that made sense to him, any he wanted to explore further and remove the ones that were irrelevant. Once this was done, he was left with three ideas that felt comfortable for where he was:

- Try to ignore my boss' anxiety, keep boosting my own positivity, and hope for the best.
- Take my boss for a drink and let him get it all off his chest to ease his anxiety.
- Talk to my boss and see if we can come up with alternative ways to deal with the sales pressure while I'm on my honeymoon.

Although Tim had enjoyed the idea of telling his boss with the greatest respect to go fuck himself, he didn't feel that the situation warranted such a severe verbal slap. Yet the very idea alone had provided enough positivity to get Tim back off the mat.

Instead, Tim decided to deliver the message implicitly by combining the three ideas left on his list. He would boost his own positivity by making his wedding a priority, spending time with his friends and looking after his health once more. But he'd also feel better if he took his boss for a drink and they tried to work together on alternative ways to alleviating the sales pressure rather than scrambling around desperately for numbers they weren't going to hit.

Finding *both/and* solutions enables us to approach situations with a holistic vision that recognizes the value of the connections between all parts. Neurologist Wolf Singer calls this "unitive thinking" and claims it is the ultimate source of creativity because it connects our rational left-brain with our intuitive right brain and moves us beyond traditional ideas that limit us to *either/or*.[10]

It also enables us to think beyond win-lose outcomes and consider win-win possibilities, which is the secret behind every clever plan to tame and turn around a bad boss. By understanding that we are all connected – with none of us more important than the other – it's easy to appreciate that zero-sum games, which, by definition, always end with a winner and a loser, carry a heavy personal, social, and business cost.

This approach, sometimes referred to as social aikido, turns the strength of your boss into your advantage by transforming an enemy into an ally. While most of us have been raised to believe that the only way to win a conflict is to neutralize, injure or eliminate our opponents, hundreds of scientific studies have shown that the use of antagonistic and adversarial tactics is more likely to escalate the intensity of a dispute. This then causes increased hostility, suspicion and distrust and an atmosphere of threats and coercion. Conflicts drag us down, devastate us psychologically, poison our relationships and interfere with our performance.[11]

Not surprisingly, win-lose encounters spark negative emotions like fear, anger, disgust, repulsion and hatred, which mobilize us to find out what is wrong in the situation and try to eliminate it. Given that our relationship with our boss has the most profound impact on our engagement, our health and our well-being at work, it makes no sense to fill our bosses with the negative emotions that are sparked by win-lose encounters.[12] Even if we're walking out the door to a new job, our colleagues still have to live on with our boss.

In contrast, win-win encounters activate an expansive, tolerant and creative mindset that signals growth opportunities are at hand. The positive feelings these outcomes activate maximize the social, intellectual and physical benefits that will accrue for you and your boss making work more enjoyable, productive and profitable for you both.

It wasn't the revenge Tim originally imagined having on his boss – which involved fantasies of retribution and his boss groveling for the chance to make it up to him – and yet, unexpectedly, it felt much better. Hopeful that he'd be able to enjoy his wedding and keep his job, Tim was able to go into the discussion with a more positive mindset that not only eased his boss' anxiety – remember those mirror neurons – but also allowed them to come up with a new plan for future sales growth which appeased head office. And to the joyous relief of his bride-to-be, Tim's mojo was back.

Coming up with win-win options to deal with a bad boss isn't always easy. To help you get started in the next section, we'll deal with the five reasons you should tell your boss to go fuck themselves and a variety of ways to use what you've been learning to create win-win outcomes for you both. Read on and see for yourself.

Questions to ask about what to do next

Grab a pen and paper and reflect on your answers to these questions as you work out how to get the outcome you want. These are only intended as thought starters, so as you get the hang of asking questions that open up possibilities, feel free to add more.

STEP 3: Connect with others to create win-win outcomes

1. If the shame of a bad boss has silenced you, it's time to reach out to someone whom you can trust and share your story. Who can provide the safety, empathy, and support required for you to tell them about both sides of the story – the victim and the hero – that you are experiencing with your boss?

2. When we reach out to other people we can count on, we instantaneously multiply our emotional, intellectual, and physical resources. Who can help you improve your chances of getting what you want by providing a positive, optimistic and innovative brain that you can bounce ideas off?

3. By emptying our minds of expectations about what will happen next or what's "supposed" to happen, we can tap our hidden knowledge to find new solutions. Given the miracle you want and the understanding of what's driving your boss, spend two minutes completing the following sentence: "To improve my job and my current relationship with my boss by five per cent I could ..."?

Remember, two heads are better than one so don't be afraid to ask for some help and suspend your logical thinking for a bit. If you get stuck, it helps to repeat this exercise each day for up to a week before you evaluate what you've got.

Try to come up with at least six options and then go over the responses and identify the ones that make sense, any you want to explore further and remove the ones that are irrelevant. If you're stuck or want more ideas before you act just keep reading. You'll also find more ideas in the next five chapters to expand your thinking.

Section B:

Five reasons to act

Chapter Four

REASON 1:
Your Boss is Making You Miserable

P ositive emotions – ranging from joy, gratitude, serenity, and interest, to hope, pride, amusement, inspiration, awe, and love – alter our mind and body in ways that can literally help us flourish. In fact, the latest scientific evidence from more than 200 studies of 275,000 people around the world tells us that positivity doesn't simply reflect success and fulfillment; it also produces it in nearly every domain of life, including work, health, friendship, sociability, creativity and energy.[1]

If the situation with your bad boss is sucking all the joy and life out of you, it's time to make it stop. This chapter shows you how you can boost your feelings of positivity and lower your experiences of negativity on the job – regardless of your boss.

Case study 4

"Oh, she wasn't that bad," Lee laughed nervously, in case his boss should suddenly appear. Lee couldn't have been more excited to start his dream job in PR the day before, but had been a little surprised to find his boss screaming obscenities down the hallways about a colleague who'd taken a message incorrectly. Still, a little yelling wasn't going to put Lee off. Although, witnessing a stapler being thrown at one of his colleagues in the afternoon, after a spelling error was discovered on a press release, had been slightly unnerving.

However, his boss later explained when they sat down for a coffee that her actions were only due to the fact that she cared enough to "teach them how to avoid making mistakes". Lee had just assumed that his boss was having a bad day.

As the weeks rolled into months, however, Lee learnt that this was the way his boss behaved most days. At first, he stayed in the job because he was sure he could win his boss over by working harder than anyone else. He tried his best and was not afraid of challenges. Surely, this was what every employer wanted? Apparently not, based on the public humiliations that Lee's boss made him suffer.

Then Lee stayed because he was no quitter. He wasn't going to just give up over one person's bad temper. After all, how much worse could it get? It turned out quite a lot, once the put-downs and intimidations started.

Why is it important to feel good at work?

More than a year later, Lee finally hit the wall; he felt overwhelmed, miserable, and helpless. His boss' unpredictable temper had left him in a state of constant anxiety and her unreasonable demands had him working all hours. Lee dreaded going to work. Left in no doubt about the depth of his incompetence, he felt sick, tired, and overwrought.

Marty Seligman taught me a lot about how negative emotions – anger, fear, contempt, and depression – seep into our entire body. But it wasn't until he introduced me to the woman he describes as the "genius of positive psychology"[2], Barbara Fredrickson from the University of North Carolina, that I really started to understand the power and application of positive emotions in my life.

Strikingly intelligent, delightfully creative, and extraordinarily kind, Barb explained that, as we saw earlier with Rachael, our brains are literally hardwired to perform at their best – not when they're negative or even neutral – but when they're positive. Barb's research has repeatedly demonstrated that positivity doesn't just change the contents of our mind, trading bad thoughts for good ones; it also changes the scope or boundaries of our psyche by broadening and building us.

Positivity opens us up to be more creative and receptive. Studies show that it literally expands our peripheral vision, allowing us to see more than we typically do. In addition, it floods our brains with dopamine and serotonin and enables us to make and sustain more neural connections so that we can organize new information, think more quickly and creatively, become more skilled at complex analysis and problem solving, and see and invent new ways of doing things. It also alters how we see our connections with others so that we look past what separates us – like racial differences – and think more in terms of we and less in terms of me.[3]

By opening our hearts and minds, positive emotions allow us to discover and build new skills, new ties, new knowledge, and new ways of being. As our positive emotions accrue, they also build up our psychological, intellectual, social and physical resources, leaving us better equipped to face life's challenges. We become more optimistic, more resilient, more open, more accepting, and more driven by purpose. What's more, we cultivate more open-minded mental habits, ignite better connections with others and improve our biological markers for health so that we can lower our blood pressure, experience less pain, have fewer colds and sleep better. [4]

Barb describes positive emotions as "glitter dust". For example, studies have found that people who express more positive emotions while negotiating business deals are more likely to gain concessions, close deals, and incorporate future business relationships into the contracts they forged than those who are more neutral or negative. It's also why so much data shows that happier employees have higher levels of productivity, produce higher sales, perform better in leadership positions, receive higher performance ratings and higher pay and enjoy more job security[5]

My favorite part of Barb's research is her discovery that positivity obeys a tipping point. She's found when we encounter at least three heartfelt positive emotional experiences that uplift us, for every heart-wrenching negative emotional experience we endure, a tipping point occurs, which predicts our ability to see new opportunities, bounce back from setbacks, connect more with others, and reach our potential.

As part of her work she also notes that appropriate negativity – that we can learn from rather than be shamed by – is a necessary ingredient in life, which keeps us grounded in reality. Barb suggests that the goal is not to banish heart-wrenching negative emotions, but to balance them with enough heartfelt, positive ones (around 3 to 1) so that they no longer leave us to languish.[6]

The good news is that science has shown that we can learn to shape and re-shape our emotions. Just like we're each born with a weight range, we also come hard-wired with varying happiness levels, which can fluctuate on a daily basis. Increasing our positivity isn't going to suddenly make an inherently grumpy person deliriously joyful all the time, rather with concerted effort – much like consistent exercise – it's possible for this person to spend more time in their upper range of happiness and over time it seems that they can even raise their baseline. [7]

We can increase our relative positivity (our "positive ratio") in three ways by:

- Increasing the numerator (the number of positive emotions we're experiencing).

- Decreasing the denominator (the number of negative emotions we're experiencing).

- Or doing both.

This doesn't mean painting on a smiling face, wishing away our problems with positive thinking, or pretending they don't exist. Rather, it's about creating moments of heartfelt joy, gratitude, peace, curiosity, hope, pride, laughter, inspiration, awe, and love that arise from how we interpret events and ideas as they unfold.[8]

To help Lee get started, we began by sharing a knowing chuckle. After hearing his story, I suggested he tell his boss to go fuck herself. As mentioned earlier, a shot of genuine amusement is a great way to inject some positive emotion.

Then, having learned that a dose of hope is also a great way to boost our positivity, I asked Lee what it was that he really wanted. When Lee imagined his miracle, he saw himself working in a new PR job with a good boss. He'd be enjoying his role, learning new things and being appreciated for his hard work. And perhaps most tellingly, Lee would have found peace with his old boss to ensure that his lesson had been learnt.

Lee and I tried to figure out what was driving his boss so that we could hatch a clever plan to overcome her and enable him to move on. After thinking about the things that fired her up – like a misspelt press release – it was pretty easy to pick up her "ticker-tape belief" that her rights were somehow being violated and therefore unleashing her anger and wrath. Suddenly, her behavior became much more understandable – not likeable, but logical – to Lee. By being able to make sense of his boss' behavior, Lee was able to reduce some of his anxiety about her unpredictability. Easing our fears is a proven way to decrease negativity.

Finally, I asked Lee: "Given the miracle you want and the understanding of what might be driving your boss, can you try to come up with at least six ways to complete the sentence: 'To have five per cent more positivity in my job I could...'"

Below, you'll find some of the ideas that we came up with.

OPTION 1: Create jolts of joy

Lee desperately wanted to undo his boss' rants of negativity and the ways in which it impacted his life. Some days, he barely sat down before his boss was screaming about something and then the whole day spiraled down into a nightmare of bad feelings. He wanted some quick fixes to put the brakes on the descent. So, based on what I'd learnt, we agreed that each good moment Lee created would help him to move upward and outward, rather than downward and inward.

What brings a smile to your face could be very different from what brings a smile to mine. It pays to understand what makes you feel good and breaks the cycle of negativity when it's getting you down. My classmate and one of the world's leading personal coaches, Caroline Miller, calls these elements "jolts of joy" and encourages her clients to have a list on hand whenever they need to take a break and recharge.[9]

For example, meditation is a proven jolt of joy, which creates in just a few simple breaths a moment of serenity to rebalance us. The latest research in neuropsychology has discovered that meditation can rewire our brains so that we experience significant changes in happiness, health, relationships, empathy and resilience.[10] Meditation can take many forms including mindful breathing, silent walking, repeating a soothing phrase to yourself, or even singing. While twenty minutes a day is ideal, even just five minutes of gentle breathing can calm your body and brain.

Another proven jolt of joy is spending time in nature. Being immersed in nature carries both fascination, in that it draws our attention to other things, and vastness, in that it provides sufficient scope and richness to fully occupy our minds and break the cycle of negative rumination. Walking through a park, along a river or beach, or climbing a mountain have been proven to be healing and restorative because these acts allow us to literally see further, expand our thinking once more and give us more to feel good about.[11]

Lee's jolts of joy included listening to a song that inspired him or filled him with awe, watching a funny clip on YouTube that made him laugh, reading a blog or an article about something new that captured his interest or reaching out to a friend to see how they were doing. He realized that if he stepped outside of the office with his iPhone, even if it meant pretending to take a phone call or a bathroom break, he'd be able to grab a few minutes to reboot from his boss' negativity.

Everyone's different when it comes to the exact events and circumstances which trigger their emotions. Jolts of joy are a great way to seed more positive emotions into your life when you most need them. What are the things that give you a jolt of joy and can easily be accessed at work to break the spell of negativity created by your bad boss?

OPTION 2: Break the grip of rumination

While the tirades that Lee was subjected to by his boss were certainly unpleasant, it was the constant rumination that followed in his head, which he found the most destructive and difficult to shake off. No matter how hard he tried, he would discover himself turning the latest round of insults over and over in his mind, examining the causes, meaning and implications from every possible angle. Of course, the more he thought about it, the worse it got.

Rumination usually causes us to become stuck in a rut of endless questions and fans the flames of negativity, leaving us overwhelmed and demoralized. Our brains are programmed so that when we dwell on negativity, we can't see the big picture and think clearly so instead we selectively call to mind more and more negative thoughts, thereby creating a downward spiral of despair and multiplying our pessimism exponentially.

The trick is to first find something that positively distracts us by demanding our full attention so that we can take our minds off our troubles. The most effective distractions absorb us fully in the activity, so that when we emerge we've cleansed ourselves of the blues and are ready to approach our challenges with a clear mind.

One proven technique to break the grip of rumination is to exercise. Go for a jog, take a swim in the ocean, head out for a bike ride or try some yoga. Exercise has been proven to reduce tension; anxiety and depression by releasing endorphins which help us combat a bad mood. It also promotes the growth of our brains by releasing brain-derived neurotropic factor (BDNF) so that we're ready, willing, and able to learn.[12]

Another popular technique is to do something for others; to switch our focus away from our own worries and connect with a sense of greater purpose. Acts of random kindness can be performed in mere seconds by letting a stranger go ahead in a grocery line or paying someone's toll. Increasingly, we can also perform them online through games like: Spark, which allows us to use our skills to help a non-profit organization out; Free Rice, which is a simple vocabulary game in which we can earn real grains of rice for people suffering from hunger; or Raise The Village, which allows us to construct a virtual village from scratch and buy virtual items such as clothing, medical supplies and food which are actually delivered to real villagers in Uganda. Evidence suggests that acts of altruism create positive feelings, happy memories, new social connections and good mental health.[13]

Distractions must be positive, not negative, if they're to help break the grip of rumination. Trying to numb ourselves through alcohol or drugs, bingeing on food, dousing ourselves in violent media or soaking in sad songs may help us escape from painful thoughts, but do little to improve our negative mood afterwards.

Barb suggests making two lists. Label one: "Positive Distractions" and the other: "Negative Distractions" and ask yourself, "What can I do to get my mind off my troubles?" Then, brainstorm the things you already do, as well as new activities you'd like to try in good and bad weather, at work, at home, or on the road. For example, positive distractions for Lee included heading out for a run, mowing the nature strip for his neighbors or playing a Sudoku puzzle online. Negative distractions for Lee included eating something high in sugar, bitching about the situation with a colleague, or tuning out by playing the game Grand Theft Auto. For each negative distraction that tempts you, come up with a positive alternative.[14]

When you're in the grip of rumination about your bad boss, how can you positively distract yourself?

OPTION 3: Cultivate optimism

Lee's boss really went to town if a mistake was made at the PR agency. On these occasions, it wasn't just the yelling and shouting that got Lee down, but the detailed list of all of his shortcomings which accompanied the abuse. Listening to these accusations, it was hard for Lee not to take them on board as a true representation of his incompetence. He feared that no matter what he did, he'd never get the hang of PR, and as a result he'd be stuck working for his bad boss forever. These were the moments when Lee could truly see no way out and was left feeling completely pessimistic that he'd ever find his way out.

Most of us have particular habits when it comes to explaining how good and bad events happen to us. It turns out there are three important dimensions that impact our explanations: personal ("me-not me"), permanent ("always-not always") and pervasive ("everything–not everything"). Optimistic explanations find permanent and universal causes of good events and temporary and specific causes for misfortune to leave us feeling more hopeful for the future.[15]

Cultivating realistic optimism has been found to help us set more goals (including tough ones – like overcoming our bad boss), put in more effort into attaining those goals and stay more engaged in the face of difficulty.[16] For example, as his boss gave Lee feedback on his clients, he could interpret it in the following ways:

Event Type	Pessimistic Explanation	Optimistic Explanation
Bad event: Annoyed client	• "Me" – It's all my fault • "Always" – They'll never use us again • "Everything" – My career is ruined	• "Not me" – I didn't have all the details • "Not always" – It's just one mistake • "Not everything" – I can do better
Good event: Happy client	• "Not me" – Just got lucky • "Not always" – It probably won't last • "Not everything" – Life will be the same	• "Me" – I worked really hard • "Always" – My skills are improving • "Everything" – I'll get a better job

Finding positive meaning is always possible. Most of the circumstances we face in life are not 100 per cent bad. So, the chance to find the good, and honestly accentuate the positive meaning in our current circumstances, is always present, even if it's simply to realize that "this too shall pass." When we reframe unpleasant and even dire circumstances in a positive way, it influences our reactions to situations and we boost the odds that positive emotions – like hope – will flow forth and prompt us to engage in active and effective coping.[17]

Being optimistic involves a choice about how you see the world. Remember, the goal is not to eliminate negativity, deny or avoid unfavorable information or try to control situations. Instead, we want to be flexible in our optimism particularly when rumination is dragging us under, but not when clear sight or owning up is actually required. [18]

Optimistic thinking promotes positive moods, vitality, and high morale by helping us to notice what's right (rather than what's wrong), giving ourselves the benefit of the doubt, trusting that we can deal with what may be happening right now and allowing us to feel hopeful about the future.

Can you find a realistic and optimistic explanation for what may be happening?

OPTION 4: Minimize the impact of your boss

If only Lee could find a way to avoid his boss, life would be so much better. He did his best to find excuses to be out of the office at every chance he got, but unfortunately, in order to do his job, he had to physically front up most days. Besides, the longer he was out the more it seemed to rile his boss, and the moment Lee was back, she was ready to pounce with new complaints. It was an exhausting game which had completely worn him down.

Dealing with negative people in our lives isn't easy, but our best options are to modify the situation, attend to it differently or change its meaning. Rather than trying to avoid our boss, these techniques neutralize negativity by extending empathy, compassion and openness to the person who is lashing out. It's a simple fact that dire interpretations create dire emotions, whilst charitable and optimistic interpretations breed positivity.[19]

For example, you can modify the situation by experimenting with how you act when you're with your boss. Think of it as a series of tests for cause and effect – of when I do this... that happens – in which your goal is to find the responses which bring out the best in your boss. It's best to start by asking some tough questions about how you behave when you're with your boss and what "ticker-tape beliefs" this may be triggering off. Are you unintentionally baiting them with your own reactions and words? Curb your tendency to respond "in kind" to nasty negativity by escalating hostilities. Instead, break the cycle by injecting compassion, hope or humor to re-frame negative messages into neutral or positive opportunities to solve problems rather than people.

We can also attend differently by trying to be open and curious about what brings out the best – rather than the worst – in our bosses. At the end of the day, we all want to feel respected, appreciated and valued – even our bad bosses. In trying to be open and curious about what's good in our boss – it may take some real effort – by asking questions, showing an interest and expressing gratitude whenever we can, we shift the focus of our relationships and allow the good things to grow in strength and significance as time passes.

Finally, as we saw in cultivating optimism, we can change the meanings that we give to situations. Maybe our bad boss wasn't sent to destroy our lives, but to teach us one of life's most important lessons – how to care for ourselves no matter what our circumstances. Could this be a personal challenge to be more mindful, less judgmental and more compassionate? Is this an opportunity for you, like the one I was given, to toughen up? Working on our own reactions in a mindful way may dampen our boss's enthusiasm for annoying us, but even if it doesn't, the skill of mindfulness that this technique develops will leave us way out in front.

Remember, when we feel that we're able to positively impact situations rather than just being at the mercy of our bad boss, our stress levels drop, our motivation rises and we're more likely to act in ways which lead to the outcomes we want.

Can you minimize, or even neutralize, the negativity of your boss by modifying your responses, shifting your focus or finding a new purpose for their unfortunate behavior?

OPTION 5: Practice kindness

Fed up with being miserable, Lee longed for just a little bit of kindness at work. Tainted by his boss' bad behavior, even Lee's colleagues acted appallingly towards each other. It was as though the whole office was contaminated with spite and ruthlessness. Pleasantries were never exchanged, thoughtful gestures were disdained and common courtesies had been banished. It seemed like very stony ground in which to plant any hope of kindness.

Yet practicing kindness – even when it's unpleasant or we expect to receive nothing in return – is in our own self-interest. Being generous and willing to share helps you to engage in seeing others more positively, feeling more connected and being more grateful. It also makes us feel more advantaged by comparison (e.g. I'm glad I'm not so overwhelmed by my job that I've forgotten how to smile) and highlights our abilities, resources, and expertise to create feelings of control over our lives. Best of all, it can jump-start a cascade of positive social consequences influencing others to like you, to appreciate you and to reciprocate when you need kindness.[20]

Doing someone else a kindness produces the single most reliable momentary increase in well-being of any positive psychology intervention that has been tested.[21] People asked to complete five acts of kindness over the course of a day report feeling much happier even several days after the exercise is over. Picking one day a week and making a deliberate and conscious point of committing five acts of kindness – be it an unexpected compliment, helping someone without being asked or buying a coffee for another – promotes our feelings of confidence, optimism and usefulness.[22]

Barb has found that becoming more aware of kindness in our lives also boosts our positivity. She asks people to "count kind-nesses" by keeping a daily tally of each and every act of kindness committed by themselves or others. By attuning us to kindness, making us more focused on others and being more alert to how we can make a positive difference, our attention shifts to those things that we can do something about and helps us to break the cycle of negativity.[23]

At first, Lee thought it would be impossible to show any kindness towards his boss. The very idea of showing her any kindness bothered him as it seemed so undeserved. But when he was able to reconcile that any kind act would be performed with the intention of rescuing himself – after all perhaps the best revenge was his own happiness – then he found it easier to consider stepping up.

How can you notice and practice more kindness? The ideal is to concentrate your efforts on one day of the week like "Kind Monday" – even if it's unpleasant or you expect to receive nothing in return except your own sense of happiness.

OPTION 6: Tell your boss

Lee wished he had the courage to just tell his boss to back off, but confrontations generally made him uncomfortable. Besides, it was unlikely that his boss was just going to turn around and say: "Of course, Lee. I didn't realize my behavior was bothering you. I'm so glad that you asked." He didn't want to give her any more ways to make him miserable.

Conversations in which opinions may differ, emotions are extreme and the stakes are high can have a huge impact of the quality of our lives. This is why most of us back away from these discussions for fear of making a challenging situation even worse. I certainly don't recommend that everyone follow my example and tell their bosses with the greatest respect to go fuck themselves (but if this is what you have your heart set on, I'll show you how to have this conversation in the next chapter). There are, however, some important principles that I used when I confronted my boss that can give you the courage and confidence to tell your boss how you're feeling and to ask for what you want.

If we really want to a have a healthy conversation about a difficult topic we must make the other person feel safe. This can be achieved by finding a shared goal so that both parties have a good reason for talking and by showing respect.[24] Remember, our goal is to practice social aikido and find a win-win outcome that liberates us all from the spiral of negativity.

Revisiting what's driving our boss and finding a way to align our miracle with their goals can be the key to making this conversation more manageable. For example, a bullying boss like Lee's has a fear of being harmed so needs to be reassured that anything we propose helps them rather than hurts them. If Lee decided to take this path he could say something like: "I'd like to talk about something that's getting in the way of my working with you. It's a tough issue to bring up, but I think it'll help us get better outcomes for your clients. Is that ok?"

Once his boss had agreed to the conversation, Lee could follow it up with: "I know that you're very busy and I can only try to begin to imagine the kind of pressure that comes with running your own agency, but sometimes in your haste I find the way you speak to me and the words you use extremely unpleasant. To perform at my best, I need to be confident in my abilities. Is there a way that we could make our interactions more positive so that instead of worrying about what's upset you I can focus all of my attention on delivering results for your clients?"

If Lee didn't ask for his boss' permission to discuss the issue first, there is a risk that by wading straight in, a boss who fears being harmed will panic that they are being ambushed and just start shouting. By asking if it's ok to talk about a tough issue, Lee provides his boss with a chance to prepare herself for the conversation. He also ensures his boss feels safe throughout by being clear about his intention for a win-win outcome to better serve his boss' clients.

Generally, bully bosses like to set a course of action so that they can try and control any risks of damage. While Lee has opened it up to his boss to find more positive ways of interacting, he should also be prepared to offer up suggestions that reinforce the fact that he means no harm to his boss. For example, Lee might suggest that to become more mindful about the way people in the office are speaking to each other that a swear jar for charity be set up.

Be careful not to lose sight of the miracle you want and be sure to induce some positivity, as suggested above, for yourself before heading in to see your boss so that your brain is functioning at its very best. Can you find a shared goal and genuine respect to help you have an honest, healthy and productive conversation with your boss?

Do you want to enjoy your job more?

Given the miracle he wanted – to be working in a new PR job and to have learnt the lesson of finding peace with his boss – Lee now had six different ways to find five per cent more positivity in his job. He could:

- Create jolts of joy to break the spell of negativity cast by his boss.

- Break the grip of rumination by embracing positive distractions when things are weighing him down.

- Cultivate optimism by finding positive meanings in good and bad events.

- Minimize his boss' impact by modifying his responses and shifting his focus towards finding a new purpose for her unfortunate behavior.

- Practice kindness by noticing and concentrating his efforts into one day of the week.

- Tell his boss that he doesn't like her behavior and find a win-win way of moving forward.

When he was done, I asked Lee to go over the responses and identify the ones that made sense to him, any he wanted to explore further and remove the ones that were irrelevant. Once this was done, Lee decided that breaking the grip of rumination and cultivating optimism would boost his positivity to make him more credible for new employers. He also decided to try practicing kindness with his boss to quiet her fear of imminent harm.

The secret Lee learned was to not grasp positivity too firmly, denying its transient nature. Rather, he focused on seeding more of it into his life. Ironically, by being able to act as though he was someone who wanted a peaceful relationship with his boss, Lee's feelings of confidence, optimism and usefulness kept increasing, making it possible for him to eventually find a much better job with a good boss. And with the deepest feeling of peace, Lee wished his bad boss – whose rampages continued – the very best of luck. It was social aikido at its best.

Barb told me that a few years ago she came across a greeting card that read: "Life gives us negativity on its own. It's our job to create positivity." She said she liked this phrasing because it reminds us that positivity is a choice – a choice we all need to make again and again, day after day. As a result of all she taught me, I'm particularly careful to gauge the balance of positivity to negativity in my life by using Barb's free five minute Positivity Test online (you'll find it at **http://www.michellemcquaid. com**). When I find it falling below three to one I use many of these strategies to improve the way I'm feeling about work.

How much positive emotion do you have in your life?

Questions to ask

REASON 1: Your boss is making your life miserable

Given the miracle you want and the understanding of what might be driving your boss, can you try to come up with at least six ways to complete the sentence: "To have five per cent more positivity in my job I could ..." Below, you'll find some of the questions to help guide you.

1. What are the things that give you jolts of joy and which can easily be accessed at work to break the spell of negativity created by your bad boss?
2. When you're in the grip of rumination about your bad boss, how can you positively distract yourself?
3. Can you find a realistic and optimistic explanation for what may have been happening?
4. Can you minimize or even neutralize the negativity of your boss by modifying your responses, shifting your focus or finding a new purpose for their unfortunate behavior?
5. How can you notice and practice more kindness – the ideal is to concentrate your efforts on one day of the week like "Kind Monday" – even if it's unpleasant or you expect to receive nothing in return except your own sense of happiness?
6. Can you find a shared goal and genuine respect to help you have an honest, healthy and productive conversation with your boss?
7. How much positive emotion do you have in your life? Take the positivity test at **http://www.michellemcquaid.com.**

When you're done, go over the responses and identify the ones that make sense to you, any you want to explore further and remove the ones that are irrelevant. Is there an idea left, or a combination of several, that you could use to overcome your bad boss?

If not, try the same exercise tomorrow and the day after that and be sure to ask people you trust for some help. I promise it will come.

Chapter Five

REASON 2:
You can't do what you do best

G lobal research organization, Gallup, has spent the past decade survey-ing more than 10 million people worldwide on the topic of employee engagement (or how positive and productive people are at work). Only one-third or 33 per cent of the people they've interviewed strongly agree with the state-ment: "At work, I have the opportunity to do what I do best every day." Further polls have found that among those who "strongly disagreed" or "disagreed" with this statement, not one single person was emotionally engaged in their job.[1]

This chapter looks at the all-important issue of workplace engagement. Are you just bored in your job or do you actually hate what you're doing? How can you create more engagement in your job so it's more enjoyable and inspiring for you? Read on, for key options on how to attain a healthy and satisfying level of engagement in your work.

Case study 5

"I hate my job," Christine confided, tears brimming in her eyes. "I dread Mondays. I despise going to the office. I spend all day doing things that bore me senseless. My boss is next to useless and just keeps getting me to do the same, stupid things. I can't believe that this is how people live their lives. It feels so wrong."

In just six months, Christine's graduate position in a global consulting firm had gone from hard-won to hard-to-put-up-with. At 28, she was one of the old-est "graduates" having discovered her love for the law later than her peers. To have it turn to dust so quickly was just devastating.

"I just don't know what to do," Christine told me. "I've advised my boss that I'm unhappy, but he doesn't seem to care. My role isn't anything like what my boss promised. I spend most of my time reading about tax law, which I barely understand. I feel like it's too soon to just quit and my boyfriend's counting on my salary to help him get through his new course.

"I've tried to suck it up and just get on with it, but every day it becomes harder and harder. We're fighting more at home. I don't enjoy spending time with friends who all keep asking how my big, fancy job is going. I feel fat and unfit because every night all I can do is flop on the couch and eat in an effort to forget about my day. I've never felt so unhappy and I can't see any way out because my boss just doesn't give a damn."

Why does engagement matter in our jobs?

Overwhelmed by her story of helplessness, Christine was spiraling down to a very dark place when we finally sat down to chat. Highly intelligent and capable, Christine had never felt so uninspired and unproductive in her life. Normally someone who brightens up any room you find her in, I'd never seen Christine so depressed.

Luckily for Christine, not too long ago, on a hot Philadelphian night, I had tasted the best gelato ice-cream of my life. What made it so good? The person whom I was eating it with, the Mick Jagger of psychology, a professor of social science at the Peter Drucker School of Business at Claremont University by the name of Mihaly Csikszentmihalyi – or "just call me Mike". How could this help Christine? Mike is famous for identifying and enhancing the concept of flow.

Flow is the feeling we have when we're one with music, time stops and we lose all self-consciousness because we're fully absorbed in what we're doing. We may not be thinking or feeling anything and yet we're learning, growing, improving and advancing so that we feel more capable, in control and satisfied afterwards. It is engagement in the fullest sense and it's an essential determinant for happiness and life satisfaction and all the benefits that they bring.[2]

Mike explained that having a clear goal that balances our strengths with the complexity of the task at hand, and a sense of autonomy, was necessary in order to attain the state of flow. It's that specific zone between under-challenged and over-challenged – between boredom and anxiety – which provides a positive and productive natural high that is intrinsically rewarding. It is the experience of working at our full capacity.[3]

One cautionary note: being in flow is not the same as losing track of time while watching television, playing video games, overeating, overspending, gambling or otherwise being unaware of our behavior. These conditions are known as "junk flow" and are not directed towards the attainment of valued and meaningful goals, but are mind-numbing activities which don't involve any challenge or skill.[4]

Unfortunately, a life without the flow of engagement, like Christine's had become, is also a recipe for misery. It leaves us feeling bored, helpless and unworthy of joyful experiences. It makes us increasingly self-absorbed and it's easier to become depressed.[5]

With Mike's advice top-of-mind, I asked Christine what a miracle that allowed her to be more engaged in her work would look like. Without hesitation, she replied: "A job that I liked. I want to go to work and feel like I'm adding value that's appreciated. I want a chance to do what I do best each day. I want to be able to learn new things and grow. And I want a boss who'll guide me on making it all happen."

As we talked further, Christine readily admitted that she'd spent more time complaining about her job in recent months than trying to find ways to be engaged in it. "But honestly," she said, "I have no idea how to make it work."

This wasn't helped by the fact that Christine had a "Laissez-Faire Boss" who made his team members do all the work so that he had nothing personally invested. He showed no interest in helping Christine find a solution to her concerns and she'd taken this as a clear sign that he didn't want to be bothered with her. In fact, it seemed whenever a team member needed him to act or take a stand, her boss would disappear into thin air in the hope that by the time he returned it would all be magically sorted. Observing these consequences and keeping in mind the boss type chart in Chapter 2, it seemed possible that Christine's supervisor may be driven by a fear of loss.

Based on these Beliefs, I wondered if perhaps it wasn't a case of not caring about Christine's unhappiness, but rather the fear of losing her from his team that was causing her boss to act so carelessly. Christine admitted that she'd never contemplated this, but it could definitely be a possibility. If it was true, maybe he wasn't the complete "asshole" Christine had assumed he was; he was just paralyzed by his fear of loss. And suddenly, a tiny glimmer of empathy and hope appeared.

Finally, I asked Christine, "Given the miracle you want and the understanding of what might be driving your boss, can you try to come up with at least six ways to complete the sentence: "To feel more engaged in my job and improve my current relationship with my boss by five per cent I could ...". After two minutes, the only answer on Christine's page was, "be nicer".

I asked Christine if being nicer to her boss would deliver the miracle she wanted and she admitted probably not. While being nicer to her boss probably wouldn't hurt – remember, even performing an unreciprocated act of kindness makes us feel better – it wasn't going to help her feel more engaged in her work. But just how could Christine make her job more interesting in spite of her boss?

OPTION 1: Discover your strengths

Christine needed a chance to go to work and do what she did best each day. It's human nature to want to feel affirmed and valued and when this is earned by applying our strengths to our tasks, these gratifications are a vital contributor to our ability to flourish and enjoy our jobs.[6] People who have the opportunity to focus on their strengths every day are six times more likely to be engaged in their jobs and more than three times as likely to report having an excellent quality of life in general.[7]

Our strengths are our pre-existing patterns of thoughts, feelings and behaviors which are noticeable for the engagement, energy and enthusiasm they generate. They might comprise our talents, interests, resources, and/or character. They're things we look forward to doing, we feel absorbed by while we're doing them and by which we feel invigorated and fulfilled after we've done them. Strengths are where our greatest successes happen and where we experience enormous growth.[8]

When we engage our strengths towards a goal that requires the completion of tasks that are neither too easy nor too hard – they're just right – we enter the magical state of flow and are able to experience pleasure and perform at our very best.[9] I asked Christine what she thought her strengths were and how she was using them at work. While she quickly came up with a long list of what they weren't, Christine had no real idea about what her strengths actually were. To help her, I suggested she take the Values in Action (VIA) Survey of character strengths – you can take it for free at **http://www.michellemcquaid.com** – to see what your strengths are.

74

After taking the test, Christine discovered that her top strengths included love, honesty, perspective, social intelligence, and creativity. It was apparent that Christine rarely, if ever, had the chance to use her strengths in her job and therefore the state of flow was largely absent from her work. Caring for others wasn't encouraged so her strengths of love and social intelligence went untapped. She felt like the tasks she was required to complete made little use of her perspective or creativity. And being honest was getting her nowhere. No wonder she hated her job.

Finding a way to use our strengths in a state of flow at work leads us to be more involved in life (rather than alienated from it), to enjoy activities (rather than to find them dreary), to have a sense of control (rather than helplessness) and to feel a strong sense of self (rather than unworthiness).[10] Incorporating them into our jobs can be something we take on alone or something that we share with our boss. Do you know what your character strengths are? Can you find ways to use them in moments of flow each day at work?

OPTION 2: Re-craft the tasks in your job

The problem Christine felt was that none of her strengths could be really fitted into her role. And she was right, they weren't obviously incorporated. So, we started to look for other ways this could occur. And we also asked the question: "What if Christine could change parts of her job so that her strengths could be more fully utilized?"

It's easy to get trapped into thinking about our job as a list of things that must be done at all costs. But says who? What if we were able to adjust what we do? Who would we start talking to? What other tasks would we take on? And who would we work with? The reality is that formal job requirements are not the only thing determining what we do.[11]

I asked Christine to think about how much time, energy, and attention she devoted to her various tasks and reflect on what was most enjoyable and what was most draining. She found that she enjoyed her interaction with other graduates who often sought her out for advice, which gave her a chance to use her strengths of social intelligence and love. She also liked pulling together new information she'd read and sharing it with others, which allowed her to use her perspective and creativity. Unfortunately, this made up about ten per cent of her work on a good day; the rest was all soul-destroying dross.

Each of us also has the latitude to feel more engaged by helping to "craft" our jobs. Crafting our jobs by changing the type and number of tasks we choose to undertake and the way we think about our work and/or who we interact with, allows us to reclaim our power, motivation and relationships. It helps us to adjust what we do every day by reframing the way we think about our jobs and where we choose to spend our time and energy.[12]

Christine couldn't just drop all the responsibilities she loathed, but she could tweak her job by 15 minutes here and there to better fit her interests, strengths and passions. For example, she could volunteer to initiate a new project for her boss that would make better use of her strengths. Or she could seek out mentors and colleagues in the firm who were doing more of the work that she wanted to spend her time on.

Re-crafting our day-to-day tasks and relationships – even slightly – to make more room for our strengths makes our work more enjoyable and engaging. You can do this discretely or have a direct conversation with your boss if you think it won't set their alarm bells off. How could you re-craft elements of your job – what you do and who you do it with – to spend 15 minutes or more doing what you do best each day?

OPTION 3: Live mindfully

Christine wasn't sure if she could re-craft her job and not get in trouble from her boss – although his laissez-faire leadership style meant it would probably take him a while to catch up. Not all roles are easily open to job crafting so another option worth considering is developing the practice of mindfulness.

Practiced in the East and the West, in ancient times and in modern societies, mindful awareness techniques help us move toward wellbeing by training our mind to focus on moment-to-moment experiences without being swept up by judgments of good or bad. Focusing our attention in this way is a biological process which promotes health – a form of brain hygiene – that frees us from the weight of negativity.[13]

Ellen Langer is a Harvard psychologist who has spent her life studying mindfulness. Her energy, interest, playfulness, accomplishments and contentment are a walking testament to the benefits. Ellen teaches her students that events do not come with evaluations; rather we impose evaluations on our experiences and, in so doing, create our experience of the event. She believes that noticing new things is the essence of mindfulness, while unquestioningly accepting a single-minded evaluation of what we see is mindless.[14]

For example, studies suggest that if Christine evaluates her job tasks as "work" she'll enjoy it less and her mind is more likely to wander as she tries to get through the tasks. But if Christine changes her mind and evaluates the same job tasks as "play" she is more likely to enjoy what she's doing and be more mindfully engaged in her work. When we view a situation mindfully we're able to generate multiply consequences that open up our choices.[15]

Since I met Ellen, I've tried to live my life more mindfully (you can find samples of mindful meditation techniques that I've found helpful at **http://www.michellemcquaid.com**), particularly in the moments that I've found myself feeling overwhelmed, fearful or stuck. In these moments, I've reached for the questions Ellen gave me to be more mindful of what else is happening around me: When was this decided? Who says so? Based on what information? With what motivation? And, suddenly as I answer these questions, hidden worlds start to open up.

The more we notice, the more we become aware of how things change depending on the context and perspective from which they are viewed. How mindfully do you pass your time at work?

OPTION 4: Tell your boss

Finally, if you've reached a place where you think nothing short of a verbal slap will wake your boss up to what you need, and you're prepared to live with the consequences – and have checked it's not legal grounds for dismissal in your organization – then by all means tell them with the greatest respect to go fuck themselves. If you want a future of any kind with your boss – be it to keep your job or obtain a reference – the way you deliver this message is of great importance.

A boss like Christine's, who has a fear of loss, needs to be reassured that although you've had enough of feeling unengaged in your job, this doesn't mean that you're severing the relationship. For example, if Christine decided to take this path she could say something like: "With the greatest respect, if you think I'm going to keep doing work that I loathe indefinitely you can go fuck yourself. However, my great preference is for us to amicably find a way to balance my workload so that I can use my strengths to bring more value to us both. Here is how I'd like to try it for the next month and then if we need to we can adjust it as you want..."

If Christine stopped after simply telling her boss to go fuck himself, all of his anxieties about losing her as a member of his team would be on high alert causing him to withdraw rather than work it through with her. By hearing that her intention is to balance her workload to bring more value to them both, her boss' laissez-faire tendencies to let others do the work are aroused. And by signaling her intention to act – just as a trial – Christine makes it easy for her boss to avoid having to make an explicit decision. After all, he can change his mind later if he's up to it.

A certain amount of levity – buoyancy and lightness – is also vital to this delivery so that our bosses don't take our swearing too seriously. Using levity to deliver our message grabs attention, relaxes the person listening so they're more receptive to our message and enhances our ability to negotiate.[16]

Christine's strengths of love and social intelligence are essential in helping her deliver this message to her boss. What strengths can you engage to help you to have a direct, respectful conversation with your boss while asking for what you need?

Do you want to be engaged in your job?

Christine decided to try the sentence stem completion exercise once more: "To feel more engaged in my job and improve my current relationship with my boss by five per cent I could..."

- Be nicer to my boss
- Try to use my strengths to create more moments of flow at work
- Re-craft the tasks and relationships around my job
- Tell my boss respectfully (and with levity) to go fuck himself and present an alternative scope for my role
- Find a different job in the firm or elsewhere

When she was done, I asked Christine to go over the responses and identify the ones that made sense to her, any she wanted to explore further and remove the ones that were irrelevant. Once this was done she decided that while she'd try to keep being a bit nicer to her boss, she'd also start to re-craft the tasks and relationships around her job to make better use of her strengths and see how things progressed.

When I checked in on Christine a while later, things were looking up. She'd stopped sniping at home, had started seeing her friends again and had signed on for a yoga class to get some balance back. She'd started subtly changing the things she was spending time on in her job and was having a lot of coffee with other people in the firm who led areas of work she preferred.

In fact, one of them had offered her a new role in the firm, but her boss – afraid of losing her – was only in agreement if she continued working for him as well. Two jobs for the price of one! Shortly after, Christine quit and has found a boss and a job she loves.

REASON 2: You can't do what you do best

Given the miracle you want and the understanding of what might be driving your boss, can you try to come up with at least six ways to complete the sentence: "To have five per cent more engagement in my job and improve my relationship with my boss I could ..." Below, you'll find some of the questions to help guide you.

1. Do you know what your strengths are? (Visit **http://www.michellemcquaid.com** for a free strengths survey.) Can you find ways to use them in moments of flow at work each day?

2. How could you re-craft elements of your job? How much time and energy do you currently spend on various tasks? What do you find the most enjoyable? What do you find the most draining? How can you spend a little more time each day doing what you do best and with the people you work best with?

3. How mindfully do you pass your time at work?

4. What strengths do you have which would help you to respectfully tell your boss to go fuck themselves, while asking for what you need?

When you're done, go over the responses and identify the ones which make sense to you, any you want to explore further and remove the ones that are irrelevant. Is there an idea left, or a combination of several, that you could use to overcome your bad boss?

If not, try the same exercise tomorrow and the day after that and be sure to ask people you trust for some help until you have an answer that gives you hope again.

Chapter Six

REASON 3:
You're damaging your relationships

Other people matter. Researchers have found that the single best predictor of momentary experiences that lead to higher well-being and engagement at work is not what we're doing, but who we're doing it with. In fact, having a best friend at work makes it seven times more likely that we're engaged in our jobs, makes us better at engaging customers, helps us to produce higher quality work, improves our well-being and makes it less likely we'll be injured on the job. Even small social interactions, like chit-chat in person, on the phone or via email, lead to large gains in production.[1]

Yet studies also show that a bad boss greatly undermines our relationships at work and at home. If a bad boss situation is slowly, but surely destroying your interactions with others, what can you do to repair and protect your relationships against a difficult superior?

Case study 6

"I don't want to discuss it any further Jen," said her boss. "I've changed the department's strategy. I don't care what you were doing before. From now on, you'll work at our other location whether you like it or not. Please go and pack up your office. I'd like to get in before the day is out."

Jen couldn't believe it. Two weeks ago, the school had restructured its management – again. Jen, who had led the career counseling services for students for the past five years, and her team of four others, suddenly found themselves with a new boss who had never counseled anyone before.

After a cursory "hello", Jen's boss had deliberately avoided the team for the first week, leaving them suspended in a vacuum of uncertainty. When she finally emerged, she had created a grand plan to reorganize the counseling services and unveiled her ideas at a team meeting to which Jen was not invited.

To top it all off, when her boss finally spoke to Jen it was to tell her that she was to move to the other campus. When Jen finally found her new office, it was actually part of the library's kitchen, buried in the bowels of an old building where students would never find her. Jen had never worked with someone who behaved so unprofessionally. What was wrong with this woman?

Why are relationships so important?

Over the coming months, Jen's new boss continued to chip away, bit-by-bit, at any sense of pleasure that she had found in her job. Stranded on an outlying campus, it was impossible for Jen to maintain the social activities, like coffee breaks with her team, lunch with departmental colleagues, or even a friendly hello to new staff, which helped her to stay connected. Unable to easily find Jen, fewer students were seeking out her services. Feeling miserable about her job, Jen found that she was less interested in spending time with her friends outside of work. She just didn't have the energy left after dealing with her boss.

It was the first weekend of my Masters of Positive Psychology class in Philadelphia and there was a heated debate underway about the statistical measures of well-being and happiness, when a learned voice called out from the back: "Surely all anyone really needs to be happy is sex and Twinkies." As the class dissolved into raucous laughter, I saw that the man who had spoken was well into his seventies, with a shock of silver hair, with broad shoulders, and a mischievous smile on his face. It was none other than George Vaillant.

George is legendary for having overseen one of the longest running psychological studies of all time – the Harvard Grant Study – which followed 268 Harvard sophomores and 456 disadvantaged inner-city youth, from their entrance into college in the late 1930s for the next 68 years of their lives. Scientists have used the wealth of data from questionnaires they completed, information from their physicians and personal interviews about their mental and physical health, career enjoyment, retirement experiences and marital quality to identify the life circumstances and personal characteristics that distinguished the happiest, fullest lives from the least successful ones. George told us that he could sum up the findings in one word: "Love".[2]

"Seventy years of evidence proved one very important thing. That our relationships with other people matter, and matter more than anything else in the world," George explained. He found out that social bonds didn't just predict overall happiness for the men in the study, but also eventual career achievement, occupational success, and income.[3]

Evolution has genetically hard-wired us for love. As children, our survival depends on unconditional and forgiving love. As adults, we flourish when the positive emotions of love, joy, hope, forgiveness, compassion and trust allow us to attach to social networks that provide cooperation, support and physical, intellectual, emotional and financial prosperity. George taught us that successful human development involves: first, absorbing love, next, reciprocally sharing love, and finally, giving love unselfishly away. In a nutshell: sex and Twinkies (love and food) is all we need for happiness.[4]

We also have a biological need for social support. Each time we joyfully connect with another person, the pleasure-inducing hormone oxytocin is released into our bloodstream, immediately reducing anxiety and improving concentration and focus. Each social connection also bolsters our cardiovascular, neuroendocrine and immune systems, so that the more connections we make over time, the better we function. In fact, research has convincingly shown that social support has as much effect on life expectancy as smoking, high blood pressure, obesity and regular physical activity.[5]

Our relationships with others are our best guarantee of lowering stress and raising well-being. Studies show that each positive interaction we have during the course of the work day actually helps return our cardiovascular system back to resting levels and over the long haul, they protect us from the negative effects of job strain. Each connection also lowers cortisol levels, which helps us recover faster from work-related stress and makes us better prepared to handle it in the future.[6]

When it comes to our jobs, research shows that positive social connections predict more individual learning behavior, motivate us more than money or power and improve our effectiveness and performance. Even brief encounters which fuel openness, energy and authenticity among colleagues – one conversation or an email exchange – can infuse us with a greater sense of vitality, giving us a pep in our step and a greater capacity to act. [7]

By the time Jen sat down and shared what was really happening with me, she was feeling isolated, resentful and helpless. "Ah Jen," I said after her story of anxiety and frustration came pouring out, "Just tell her to go fuck herself." After a moment of shock, Jen's face broke into a huge smile as she laughed, "I can't do that!"

I pressed on: "If you could wake up tomorrow and head into work to find that a miracle occurred overnight, what would be different? Really think about it, Jen. How would you know the miracle happened? What would you be doing? How would your boss be behaving? What would feel it like?"

When Jen imagined her miracle she was still working in her job, but as a valued member of the team again. Meetings were scheduled for when she could attend. She could find time to spend at the old office to connect and catch up. And she had a relationship with her boss that was built on respect. That sounded reasonable enough, but Jen admitted it probably wasn't the way she had been behaving.

Jen understood intuitively that her boss was a bit of a "control freak", but she wasn't sure how to manage this insecurity so that she could create the outcome that she longed for. As we talked about Jen's boss' worst behaviors, it became clear that she was an "Authoritarian Boss" who likes to micromanage for fear that something bad may happen. Her efforts to implant a new strategy and insert herself in the middle of the team in Jen's office was perhaps her way of ensuring that nothing terrible would occur.

"So, Jen," I said, "Given the miracle you want and your understanding of what might be driving your boss, can you try to come up with at least six ways to complete the sentence: "To improve my relationships with my colleagues and my boss by five per cent I could....". Here are some options we thought were worth a try.

OPTION 1: Respond actively and constructively

Now that Jen spent less time with her colleagues and peers she was finding it harder to experience those moments of connection that happen naturally over lots of coffees. She was missing the little details of people's lives and consequently was losing touch with the things that were most important for them. Some of her relationships at work were starting to become stilted and awkward. It made Jen feel sad and left out.

We all know that an important part of maintaining a social bond is being there, both physically and emotionally, especially when someone is in need. But, an interesting new body of research suggests that how we support people during good times, more than bad times, affects the quality of our relationships. That is, when someone shares news of a victory or just a good thing that's happened to them, how you respond can either build the relationship or undermine it.[8]

For example, if a team member tells you they've just had four weeks of holiday leave approved so they can travel to Italy you might say:

- "OK. Have you finished that report yet?" – This is a passive and destructive response. There is no real effort to engage with their news and we've turned to a subject that's likely to kill off any positive emotions. People responding in this way often show no expression, use little eye contact and may physically turn away to show their disinterest in the other person's good news.

- "How will you keep up with all your deadlines with so much time away?" – This is an active and destructive response. We've made an effort to engage with their news, but we've done it in a way that induces anxiety and is likely to ruin their good mood. People responding in this way often frown and look worried as they try to play devil's advocate by talking about the problems.

- "That's great." – This is a passive and constructive response. We've still made no real effort to engage, but we've acknowledged that something good has happened for them. People responding in this way often use no expression or smile slightly.

- "How wonderful! When will you leave? Whereabouts in Italy will you go?" – This is an active and constructive response. We've made an effort to engage with their news and we've done so in a way that they can keep savoring and building positivity. People responding in this way smile and use eye contact to display enthusiasm and excitement.

When we take delight in other people's windfalls or successes by asking questions that appreciate and validate their good fortune, we are responding actively and constructively. It is a positivity boost for both parties and research shows that it enhances relationship commitment and satisfaction and fuels the degree to which people feel understood, validated, and cared for during a discussion – all of which improves our depth of social connection. [9]

Given my love of experimenting with and applying what I learn, I can unequivocally vouch that this technique really works. One night, on a date with my husband, exhausted after a full day of work and wrangling kids, he started to enthuse about his latest and greatest technology project at work. Longing for a good night's sleep and lacking my conversational best, I deliberately used active-constructive responses: "Wow. What are you looking forward to most about the project?" And: "It sounds great. Who is the most interesting person you'll work with?"; and so on for the next half an hour. Interestingly, as the conversation continued, I noticed not only was he buzzing, but that I was starting to feel more energized as well. While the technology didn't interest me in the least, hearing about his interests and hopes picked me right up. His verdict later that night as we were brushing our teeth: "Tonight was one of the best conversations we've ever had."

Jen realized that by asking people, "What's gone well lately?" when she caught up for briefer chats, she could prompt them to share some good news and then make the effort to respond actively and constructively to try to maintain their social bonds. Who knows, maybe it might even help her find a way to connect with her boss?

Could you make more effort to ask questions and take a positive interest when people share their good news? What impact could this have on your relationships?

OPTION 2: Create connection rituals

Jen found one of her biggest challenges was just finding the time to maintain her relationships with colleagues. The travel between campuses meant it wasn't practical for her to visit her old team more than twice a week and technically she was only meant to do this for legitimate reasons, like a meeting called by her boss. She tried to stay connected with emails and phone calls, but as the weeks had gone by, she found it harder and harder to find the time to keep up. No wonder she felt lonely and isolated.

Unfortunately, relationships don't just happen – they're made and maintained by our efforts and actions. One of the best ways to nurture our relationships at work is to create rituals which allow us to get together and be in touch with people we value on a regular basis.[10] For example, Jen could identify a couple of colleagues with whom she'd like to stay in close contact and invest more time into their relationships now that she's in the office less frequently. It could be a weekly, fortnightly or monthly coffee catch up, an online game of scrabble, or a regular professional learning opportunity. In this way, these important colleagues become as much a priority as all the other areas of Jen's work. If you give this a try, don't feel the need to control all the interactions – ask your colleague what they'd like and make sure you give them space when required.

To inspire us to find the time to create rituals which prioritize connecting with others, studies show when we get at least six hours of daily social time, it increases our well-being and minimizes stress and worry. The six hours can include time at work, at home, on the telephone, talking to friends, sending emails and other communication, but each hour of social time we accumulate quickly decreases the odds of having a bad day. Even three hours of social time reduces the chances of having a bad day to 10 per cent. And each additional hour of social time – up to about six hours – improves the odds of having a good day and minimizing the negativity of our bad boss. [11]

Making time to maintain our relationships at work fills us with positivity. In turn, these enhanced feelings of happiness help us to attract more high-quality interactions, which will make us even happier, and so on, in a continuous upward spiral toward flourishing.[12]

Are there connection rituals you can create which will help you strengthen valued relationships at work?

OPTION 3: Show appreciation

Jen felt that her relationships at work had also been damaged by the negativity that she'd been exhibiting since her boss arrived. When she did catch up with colleagues, all that seemed to come out of her mouth were complaints. Even Jen was sick of hearing herself whining and criticizing, but she just didn't seem able to stop. It was very out of character for Jen to be so self-obsessed and she longed to get back to the more positive and enjoyable conversations of her past.

Practicing appreciation and gratitude is a kind of mega strategy to improve our levels of positivity and our relationships. It opens our heart and urges us to give back – to do something good in return – helping to nurture new relationships and improve existing ones. Perhaps this is why countless studies have shown that consistently grateful people are more energetic, emotionally intelligent, forgiving, and less likely to be depressed, anxious, or lonely.[13]

Expressions of gratitude at work have been proven to strengthen both personal and professional bonds. As researchers have found, the absence of close friendships at work can lead to boredom, loneliness and depression. Showing our appreciation for a colleague is an easy way to spark an upward spiral of relationship growth where each individual feels motivated to strengthen the bond.[14]

For example, Jen could set herself the goal of reaching out to thank at least one of her colleagues each week for something they have done which helped her out. It doesn't really matter if she sees them, calls them or emails them, as long as she is specific in her appreciation for what they did and the effort that was put in. When I had a team at work test this gratitude approach out, they were amazed to find that not only did it help them focus on how much others were helping them, but that a tidal wave of unprompted appreciation was returned.

People who have at least three or four very close friendships at work are healthier, have higher well-being and are more engaged in their jobs. Could creating a habit of showing your appreciation for colleagues help to improve your relationships at work?

OPTION 4: Avoid social comparisons

Worst of all, Jen found that the more unhappy and negative she became, the more preoccupied she was with comparing her lot to others in the team. Ken was being allowed to represent the department at a conference she really wanted to attend. Sandy didn't seem to have as many students to counsel as the rest of them. Everything that Kym suggested to their boss seemed to be the world's greatest idea. The more she noticed how much everyone else was getting, the more distant Jen felt from her team. She hated that she was fixating on these comparisons with her colleagues, but she just didn't seem able to stop.

Comparing ourselves to others is pretty natural. It's hard not to notice whether our co-workers are brighter, richer, healthier, funnier, or more attractive than we are. Sometimes, these comparisons inspire us to strive for ambitious goals or make us feel better about our own choices. However, most of the time observations of how others are doing or about what they have can leave us feeling vulnerable, threatened and insecure.[15]

Unfortunately, the more social comparisons we make, the more likely we are to encounter unfavorable contrasts because no matter how successful, wealthy, or fortunate we become, there's always someone who can best us. We can't be envious and happy at the same time, which is why people who spend too much attention comparing themselves to others often feel inferior, distressed and resentful and suffer a loss of self-esteem.[16]

A three-step approach can be used to shake off social comparisons. Firstly, we need to identify a recent event where the social comparisons we've made left us feeling jealous or unhappy and spend a few minutes writing about the event and what it was that unsettled us so we can unburden ourselves of any negativity. Then, we need to identify at least three things we're currently doing or could begin doing to find peace around this perceived short-coming to improve our mood and self-regard. Finally, we need to learn to avoid social comparison in the future by noting down the situations (places, times and people) that appear to trigger these insecurities and try to avoid these situations or modify them just enough to thwart their ability to unsettle us.

For example, Jen could begin by noting that when their new boss gave team members something – be it conference tickets or attention – she felt jealous and left out. She could then note that by trying to improve her relationship with her boss, explicitly asking her boss for opportunities and showing her appreciation when things are done for her, there's a genuine chance that she may also be given things in the future. Finally, rather than noting what everyone else has, Jen could decide that when these negative thoughts arose, she would focus on what she has.

The good news is that the happier we are, the less attention we pay to how others around us are doing. Are you damaging your relationships by incessantly comparing yourself to others? Can you shake off your ruminations?

OPTION 5: Tell your boss

Jen wished she could tell her boss to go fuck herself, but it was language she would never use. Besides, she wasn't quite sure how it would align with her miracle. Instead, she decided to think about what an honest conversation that allowed her to find a win-win outcome might sound like with her boss. Her goal was to try and put social aikido into practice.

In order to make her superior feel safe, it will be important for Jen to remember that the fear that something bad may happen is what drives the worst behavior in her boss. As Jen wanted to stay in her job and be a more valued team member, it should be reasonably easy to align her miracle with her boss' goal to do succeed.

With a light tone and gentle smile, Jen's conversation might go something like: "I appreciate that with the move to the new location you've relieved me of many team duties so that I could find my feet. Now that I'm feeling settled, I'd really like to support you in making your strategic plan successful. Is there anything extra I could do again that might help you and the team?"

To avoid arousing any fear that something bad may happen, Jen will need to choose words that don't communicate threats or blame. Due to her boss' preference to micromanage tasks, it's also crucial that Jen allows her boss to select ways that she can be more involved in the team rather than being too eager to offer suggestions or dictate outcomes.

It's also critical Jen remembers that our emotions are enormously contagious due to the mirror neurons in our brains. By smiling in a relaxed, calm, non-threatening way as she delivers her message, her boss' amygdala – the almond shaped part of our brain that is largely responsible for both the creation of emotions and the memories they generate – primes her to feel the same allowing her to think in more positive and creative ways about the request that Jen has made.[17]

Mirror neurons are often right next to motor neurons in the brain, so copied feelings lead to copied actions. For Jen to accomplish the next step towards her miracle, she must be mindful of the emotions – for both herself and her boss which will help her achieve the kind of relationship she wants.

Which emotions and mirror neurons do you most want to trigger when you seek out a direct conversation with your boss?

Do you want to improve your relationships at work?

Given Jen's miracle and what we'd come to understand was driving her boss, our final attempts at her sentence stem completion looked something like this:

90

"To improve my relationships with my colleagues and my boss by five per cent I could...".

- Respond actively and constructively to more people at work.
- Create connection rituals.
- Practice showing appreciation.
- Avoid social comparisons.
- Tell my boss I'd like more opportunities to support her and the team.
- Look for a new job.
- Hope for a new boss.

When she was done, I asked Jen to go over the responses and identify the ones which made sense to her, any she wanted to explore further and to remove the ones that were irrelevant. Once this was done, she decided to ask her boss for more opportunities to support her and the team, while creating some new connection rituals with colleagues and working harder to avoid social comparisons.

As the days went on, Jen often still found herself challenged by the way her boss was treating her and the team. Many of the choices her boss made still seemed ludicrous, but being able to make sense of them more quickly ensured that they sent Jen into less of an emotional tailspin. She also became much better at heading off future threats from her boss and teaching the team to manage her superior's anxiety rather than triggering off their own set of "ticker-tape beliefs". And slowly, little by little, things seemed to calm down so that Jen's work became much more enjoyable again. And six months later, Jen's boss lost her job. Karma?

REASON 3: Your relationships are being damaged

Given the miracle you want and the understanding of what might be driving your boss, can you try to come up with at least six ways to complete the sentence: "To improve my relationships with my colleagues and my boss by five per cent I could....". Below, you'll find some of the questions to help guide you.

1. Could you make more effort to ask questions and take a positive interest when people share their good news? What impact could this have on your relationships?

2. Are there connection rituals you can create which will help you strengthen valued relationships at work?

3. Could creating a habit of showing your appreciation for colleagues help improve your relationships at work?

4. Are you damaging your relationships by incessantly comparing yourself to others? Can you shake off your ruminations?

5. Which emotions, mirror neurons and actions do you most want to trigger when you seek out a direct conversation with your boss?

When you're done, go over the responses and identify the ones which make sense to you, any you want to explore further and remove the ones that are irrelevant. Is there an idea left, or a combination of several, that you could use to overcome your bad boss?

If not, try the same exercise tomorrow and the day after that and be sure to ask people you trust for some help until you have an answer that gives you hope again.

Chapter Seven

REASON 4:
Your work seems pointless

Most of us long to be more than the sum of the tasks we perform and yet, for many of us, finding meaningful work feels like something we just can't afford. However, when a sense of meaning is found in our jobs, a growing body of evidence shows that we're happier, more motivated, more committed, and more satisfied, which enables us to perform better.[1]

This chapter explores job meaning – we all need it for our own well-being and happiness, not to mention our productivity. What's more, we can bitterly hate and resent our bosses if our jobs lack that meaning. So, how can we more closely tie our jobs to our personal values and goals?

Case study 7

"I don't understand," Belinda said. "How can half a million dollars be missing from our bank account? We were counting on reinvesting some of that profit to deliver the new services we've promised to our clients."

Belinda was on the phone to her boss, the sole owner of a burgeoning business providing accounting firms with professional development and support services. He calmly advised Belinda that he'd taken the money to use for something else he was involved with, but not to worry as he knew this would be a great learning opportunity for her to become even more innovative.

It was the last straw.

Why does meaning matter in our jobs?

Belinda loved her job because she honestly believed that what she did somehow mattered. All of these accountants were supporting 'Mom and Pop' businesses

– the backbone of local economies – and she got to help make them even better. Belinda liked hearing about their business hopes, and training, coaching, and supporting them to make a difference for their clients. She believed in what they were trying to do and genuinely wanted to help.

Our need to have meaning in our work was brought home to me the first time I met Tal Ben-Shahar, Harvard's first positive psychology lecturer. An avid sportsman who's thoughtful, insightful and courageous, Tal consults and lectures around the world to executives in multi-national corporations on leadership, ethics, happiness, resilience, goal setting and mindfulness. He stood up in front of our financially driven leadership team and convinced them that meaning was an essential requirement for productive and profitable work. It was quite something.

There is a universal need to feel that we matter, that our suffering and our hard work aren't futile. We also want to believe that we have a sense of control over our fates. This is due to the fact that we have to be able to justify our actions: why we should forgive, what we have to be grateful for, why we show kindness and so on. We long for a reason to feel connected to others. Meaning fuels our sense of self-worth and allows us to belong to something that is bigger than ourselves.[2]

Tal explained that different people find meaning in different things. In order to experience a sense of purpose, the goals we set for ourselves need to be intrinsically meaningful. They must be personally significant and in accordance with our own values and passions rather than dictated by our family, friends, workplaces or society. For example, an investment banker who finds meaning and pleasure in her work – who is in it for the right reasons – leads a more fulfilling and meaningful life than a monk who is in his field for the wrong reasons.[3]

When Belinda's boss made it clear that he was much more interested in lining his own pockets than improving their clients' lives, he ripped out the sense of purpose she associated to her work. Belinda understood that what she did probably wouldn't change the world, but she had believed that by helping small accounting firms – and the Mom and Pop businesses they served – to do what they did better that she was helping to create more prosperity for thousands of families around the country. But the idea that Belinda worked so hard just to make some rich, old guy even wealthier was abhorrent to her. The very idea made her shudder.

Since their fateful phone call, Belinda was finding it almost impossible to drag herself to work. She had no energy when she got there for the growing mountain of tasks that needed to be completed. And as her interest plummeted, her efforts had become increasingly haphazard. She knew that she was spreading misery right around the small office as the weight of depression settled across her chest. And at home, she was becoming increasingly difficult to live with. The worst part was she couldn't just quit. She needed her salary to live and couldn't keep hopping from job-to-job; it hadn't even been two years in this role.

Distressed by the idea that she was stuck in a job with no purpose, Belinda called me for a long chat and a cup of peppermint tea. You probably won't be surprised by now that my first instinct was to find a way for Belinda to own her own story by ascertaining how things would be different if she could have anything she wanted when it came to her job and the relationship with her boss.

Belinda's miracle – like most of us – was pretty straightforward. She wanted to believe that her job somehow mattered; that all the effort, sweat and hard work not only earned her a pay check, it made life a little better for someone, somewhere. And she wanted to be led by a boss who inspired and appreciated her efforts.

Although her boss' attempts at inspiration and appreciation had always been a bit slap dash prior to the money being taken out, Belinda had felt that this was the reality of her current job. And while she'd chosen to focus on the best of his efforts and tried to ignore the rest in the past, now everything he did seemed colored by his act of greed and selfishness. And Belinda was unable to disguise her disgust whenever he came into the office.

Acutely aware of the costs to herself, her work and her colleagues and to the people she loved outside of her job; Belinda begrudgingly accepted that the current story of her villainous boss was taking her further away from the miracle she longed for. While agreeing that he had behaved thoughtlessly, I asked her to think if there could be any other factors which could be driving her boss' behavior.

At first, Belinda had trouble seeing beyond the highly confident, successful and selfish person that her boss clearly was. So, I asked her why would someone with so much, need to hoard it all for themselves? Surely someone with all that capability, experience and opportunity wouldn't need to behave so selfishly?

"You know what," Belinda said, "secretly, underneath it all, I don't really think he believes he is good enough. It's why he steals my ideas, complains that I'm not innovative enough, and takes all the rewards for himself. He doesn't believe any of it will last. It's like some kind of fluke and he's scared that he'll be found out. What a horrible way to live your life." Aha!

With a glimmer of empathy found for her Narcissistic Boss, Belinda was able to wrestle back ownership of her story. So, I asked her: "Given the miracle you want and the understanding of what might be driving your boss, can you try to come up with at least six ways to complete the sentence: "To improve the meaning in my job and my current relationship with my boss by five per cent I could…".". Below, you'll find some of the ideas that we shared to help Belinda put the meaning back into her work.

OPTION 1: Finding purpose in little tasks

Demoralized by the futility of her work, Belinda had become despondent about her role. Making sales, preparing conferences and managing technology all seemed small and pointless when the purpose was just to line her boss' pockets. But researchers have found that even the smallest tasks can be imbued with greater meaning when they are connected to personal values and goals.

One way that this can be achieved is to rewrite a "job description" into a "calling description" by turning a piece of paper horizontally and on the left-hand side writing down a job task that feels devoid of meaning. Then ask: What is the purpose of this task? What will I accomplish? Draw an arrow to the right and write this answer down. If what's written still seems unimportant, ask once more: what does this result lead to?

Draw another arrow and write it down and keep working through this process until there is a result that is meaningful to you so it's possible to see the sum of the tasks.[4]

For example, Belinda might start with the task of overseeing the technology team. The purpose of the task is to keep their technology functioning so that clients can access the resources that have been prepared. That's all very nice, but probably doesn't give Belinda a reason to hop out of bed. So, what does this result lead to? It means that the clients have the support and tools that they need to be more successful. That's good, but I'm not sure Belinda will really care. So, what does this result lead to? If the accountants they help are more successful, then their clients – the Mum and Dad businesses – will be bettered served. Belinda might like the sound of that, but just in case it's not enough – what does this result lead to? It directly results in more small businesses putting food on the table for the millions of people that they employ. Now, that sounds worthwhile.

That may sound farfetched, but it's the type of thinking that helps almost one-third of hospital janitors, whose job it is to sweep the floors, dust, and empty the wastebaskets, to see their tasks as a calling to help people recover from illness by ridding the hospital of dangerous germs. It makes their job not only more bearable, but also more enjoyable.[5] After all, how many of us go to work each day and do something that could save someone's life?

The more we can align our daily tasks with our personal values, the more likely we are to find meaning in our work. By making these larger connections, our mundane tasks not only become more palatable, but we perform them with far greater dedication and see greater returns in our performance as a result.

Do you have a clear understanding of the purpose that sits behind the small tasks that comprise your role?

OPTION 2: Re-craft the purpose of your job

With the ring of a phone, Belinda's work had gone from a calling to a job because her beliefs had changed about what she was able to achieve at work. Hundreds of interviews with workers in all sorts of roles have found that we either view our work as a job (a chore we have to complete for the pay check), a career (an opportunity to advance and succeed) or a calling (something that provides meaning and purpose). Not surprisingly, when we see our work as a calling we find what we're doing more fulfilling, work harder at it and are generally more likely to be rewarded accordingly.[6]

I think this idea is best explained with the well-known story of three men who are found smashing boulders with iron hammers. When asked what they are doing, the first man said, "Breaking big rocks into little rocks." The second man said, "Feeding my family." The third man said, "Building a cathedral." In fact, what the hundreds of interviews showed is that how we view and feel about our jobs has as much to do with our beliefs as any actual work that's being done.

This meant that unless she wanted to, Belinda didn't need to quit, to change her job or go off to find herself. Instead, by practicing the skill of job-crafting, which we were introduced to earlier, she could find new possibilities opened up for the meaning of her work.

Belinda had started to think of her job as a list of things which must be done at all costs, according to her boss. But he was crying out for innovation, so maybe this was the perfect opportunity for her to take some calculated risks and re-craft her job by asking three crucial questions: What gives me meaning? What gives me pleasure? What are my strengths? She could then pay close attention to the trends that emerge.

Following the format created by Tal [7], Belinda's list may look something like this:

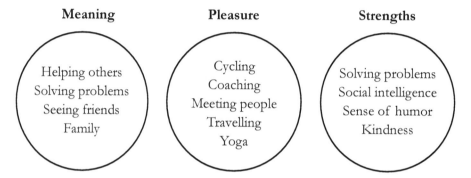

Meaning

Helping others
Solving problems
Seeing friends
Family

Pleasure

Cycling
Coaching
Meeting people
Travelling
Yoga

Strengths

Solving problems
Social intelligence
Sense of humor
Kindness

Now, which of these answers overlap for Belinda?

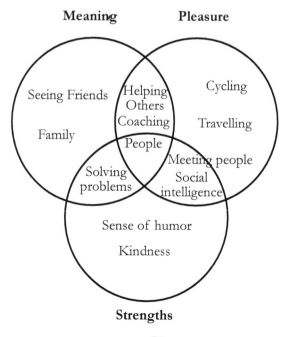

Meaning   **Pleasure**

Seeing Friends   Helping Others   Cycling

Family   Coaching   Travelling

People   Meeting people

Solving problems   Social intelligence

Sense of humor

Kindness

Strengths

In looking at the second diagram, it's clear that more her work can involve meeting and helping others through coaching and problem solving, the more meaningful Belinda will find her role. So how would Belinda's work change if she decided that this was going to be her primary focus?

When she thought about where her time, energy and attention was currently devoted, Belinda was surprised at how many of the tasks she'd already crafted to support her new goal. She could see opportunities to reprioritize some tasks and tweak others, but on the whole it turned out that what gave her a sense of meaning and what made her company successful were really not that far apart.

The bigger challenge she discovered was centered around her relationships. Spending time with her boss had a tendency to bring on bouts of disillusionment, because he only seemed interested in helping himself, which was understandable given his fear that he wasn't really good enough. On the other hand, spending time with their clients left Belinda feeling inspired and appreciated. Perhaps she needed to get out of the office more and view her clients as a kind of "virtual" leadership team that she was working for.

Re-aligning our day-to-day tasks and relationships – even slightly – to make more room for our passions can open us up to finding our calling. Align these to your interests and strengths and you'll ensure that your job becomes more enjoyable and engaging.[8] Just the thought of focusing on and getting feedback from people she respected enabled Belinda to start re-envisioning the purpose of what she was doing.

How can you re-craft elements of your job – what you do and who you do it with – to spend more of your time fulfilling a passion?

OPTION 3: Pursuing goals with purpose

If Belinda felt unable to find meaning in small tasks or incapable of re-crafting her job, an easy alternative would be to make sure she is pursuing at least one goal at work that is authentic, harmonious and within reach. The proper role of goals is to liberate us in the here and now so that we can enjoy the journey, not just the result. Goals are a means, not just an ends.

But when it comes to boosting our sense of meaning at work, it pays to pick the right kind of goals. For example, if Belinda chooses to focus on a goal that involves growth, connection and contribution – her intrinsic motivations – rather than a goal that involves money or popularity – her extrinsic motivations – then her goals will be more meaningful because they reflect her personal values rather than the need to impress others. And goals that Belinda chooses to pursue because they're interesting and personally important – she wants to do them – rather than goals that feel forced or pressured – she has to do them – are a means for meaning and pleasure in and of themselves.[9]

By injecting her days with activities which advance her towards more of her "want-to" goals, Belinda can increase the base level of her well-being at work. How meaningful her job becomes depends to a large degree on the ratio of "want-tos" to "have-tos" at work and this will determine whether she can look forward to getting up in the morning or remain exhausted at the thought of what lies ahead.

One way Tal showed me of finding some "want-to" goals to start seeding into work is to think about all the things that we can do. Out of those, select the ones we want to do. Then, reduce our choice further by zooming in on what we really want to do. Finally, select those things that we really, really want to do – and then do them.[10]

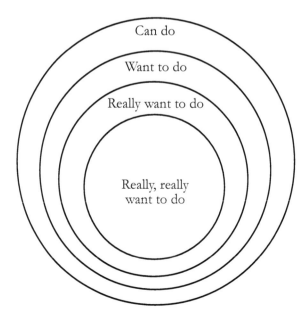

Can do

Want to do

Really want to do

Really, really
want to do

Once Belinda is clear about the type of goal that she really, really wants to do, because it will bring her a sense of meaning and joy, she needs to find a way to shrink it into smaller, more manageable, concrete steps, which will build her confidence. Then, she'll need to set out where, when and how actions about what she'll do (e.g. I will talk to one client every morning), rather than vague promises of what she'll try to stop (e.g. I'll spend less time with my boss). A critical element here is to anticipate obstacles (like boredom, lack of time, her boss' disapproval) and to think of strategies to manage them (e.g. mix it up, set aside time first thing in the morning, prepare your boss). And finally, she'll need to carry out her plan and monitor and celebrate each little success to give her a sense of progress and keep her committed to the task at hand.[11]

Realizing authentic goals satisfies our true values and innate needs, making us happier, healthier and willing to work harder. Is there one authentic, meaningful goal that you really, really want to do and could legitimately pursue at work?

OPTION 4: Tell your boss

But if all of this feels too soft, there is always the option of verbally slapping your boss and asking for what you need. Narcissistic bosses, like Belinda's, have a fear that they are not good enough so if this conversation reinforces their sense of short-coming or failure, then they'll sulkily withdraw and you'll get no further. It's very important that people with this belief don't feel attacked, but instead feel appreciated and valued for all that they bring.

For example, if Belinda sought out this conversation she could say something like: "With the greatest respect and appreciation for the thriving company you've built up, I'm finding my job lacking in meaning. I know that when you started this business you wanted to help small accounting firms do great things for their clients and you worked so hard alongside our clients to make this a reality and as a result the business has done incredibly well.

"Now, you're absolutely right about our challenge to innovate, so I've decided to follow in your footsteps by spending more of my time out with our clients so that we can keep finding new ways to grow. Here's a list of the clients I'll start with, but I'd welcome your ideas on others that should be on here as well."

By acknowledging her boss' vision ("you wanted to help..."), effort ("you worked so hard...") and success ("done incredibly well), Belinda is helping her boss to feel respected and valued so that he doesn't withdraw into his shell. In addition, Belinda is telling her boss that she appreciates his wisdom ("you're absolutely right...") and is inspired by his actions ("follow in your footsteps...") to achieve the growth they both desire. And in case he has withdrawn, despite her careful delivery, she has laid out a plan which allows her to move forward to achieving a more meaningful shared goal – helping others through coaching and use of her social intelligence.

This conversation will require Belinda to put aside all the complaints that she has about her boss for a moment and instead search for what she genuinely appreciates about him. Why? Because gratitude is an antidote to negative emotions, a neutralizer of hostility, worry, and irritation and Belinda will need to shift these in order to authentically engage in this conversation to try to trigger a win-win outcome. Studies show that expressions of gratitude at work spark an upward spiral of relationship growth where each person feels motivated to strengthen their bond.[12] And, think of all those mirror neurons busily at work for the both of you!

Fortunately, when we take the time to look, it's usually possible to find something good in everyone. For Belinda, thinking back to why she came to work for her boss was fertile ground to find things to be grateful for.

Can you find genuine things you appreciate in your boss – even if it's very small – so that when you tell them you're looking for more meaning in your work, you don't trigger off their feelings of despair or worthlessness?

Are you ready to create meaning in your job?

At the end of our discussion, Belinda's page looked like this: "To improve meaning in my job and my current relationship with my boss by five per cent I could...".

- Find meaning in small, everyday tasks.

- Re-craft my job around spending more time with our clients to feel inspired and appreciated.

- Introduce at least one meaningful, "want-to" goal to bring some balance to all the "have-to" tasks which are bringing me down.

- Tell my boss that I'm lacking meaning in my work and suggest that I spend more time innovating with clients.

- Take a formal course in coaching so that once complete, I can change jobs to something I find more rewarding.

- Find another job with a boss who has a clear sense of purpose other than just making money.

When she was done, I asked Belinda to go over the responses and identify the ones which made sense to her, any she wanted to explore further and to remove the ones that were irrelevant. Once this was done, she decided that she'd try to re-craft her job more around working with their clients so she'd spend less time with her boss, to take a formal course in coaching and to start keeping her eye out for new jobs with better bosses.

By re-crafting her job and undertaking some meaningful study, Belinda was able to enjoyably – for the most part – continue in her job for another nine months before she found a role with a more inspiring boss. Best of all, Belinda was able to take what she'd learnt about herself and her skill for job crafting to her new role, where she continues to fine tune the balance of "want-tos" and "have-tos" to find her calling steeped in meaning and pleasure.

Questions to ask

REASON 4: Your work seems pointless

Given the miracle you want and the understanding of what might be driving your boss, can you try to come up with at least six ways to complete the sentence: "To have five per cent more meaning in my job I could ..." Below, you'll find some of the questions to help guide you.

1. Do you have a clear understanding of the purpose that sits behind the small tasks that comprise your role?

2. How can you re-craft elements of your job – what you do and who you do it with – to spend more of your time fulfilling a passion?

3. Is there one authentic, meaningful goal that you really, really want to do and could legitimately pursue at work?

4. Can you find genuine things that you appreciate in your boss so that when you tell them to respectfully go fuck themselves, you don't trigger off their feelings of despair or worthlessness?

When you're done, go over the responses and identify the ones which make sense to you, any you want to explore further and remove the ones that are irrelevant. Is there an idea left, or a combination of several, that you could use to overcome your bad boss?

If not, try the same exercise tomorrow and the day after that and be sure to ask people you trust for some help until you have an answer that you're ready to act on.

Chapter Eight

REASON 5:
You're not making any progress

One of the keys to a fulfilling life is making progress toward our goals. We are all creatures of progress – we are made to grow and learn – and it's a key way in which we keep evolving. And, if we don't feel like we're progressing at work and are stagnating instead, our well-being suffers so we become bored, restless, frustrated and ultimately unproductive.

This chapter explores achievement – the sense that we're making progress towards something we value by reaching our goals, improving our weaknesses and turning failures into success. So, how can we maintain a sense of progress when we feel as if our bosses or our jobs are holding us back?

Case study 8

"I understand that you'd like to expand beyond your role in operations, but for now I need you to just keep doing what you do best. It'll happen one day, just not yet," said James' boss. This could have been a reasonable request except that for the past six months, James' boss had been promising to help find him a new role to no avail.

James had joined the national retailer three years ago with great anticipation. He'd been longing to get into retailing for years. As an experienced leader in large-scale operations, it was the most logical place to start and then his plan was to branch out into more business-orientated roles. After all, the retailer was renowned for its flexibility in helping people to diversify their career path.

Then, James did a great job for his boss and somehow he was still in the same role years later, bored out of his skull and completely stuck. He could do his work with his eyes closed. He'd tried to apply for several other roles in the company, but suspected that without his boss' support it wasn't going to happen. James did his best to stay positive and optimistic, but now his boss was inventing "behavioral problems" where none previously existed. It just wasn't fair.

James was someone who always believed in owning his own story. He'd learnt early on that stories of victims, villains, or helplessness left you stranded. And he felt clear about the miracle he longed for: an exciting, challenging, new business role within the retailing giant that his boss wished him all the best for. What mattered most to James was the sense of accomplishment – that winning feeling – that would distinguish him as someone who counted. It was his dream to be a highly respected, successful business executive.

He tried his best each day to behave as though his dream was what he wanted and attempted to show kindness to his boss even when feeling frustrated. He endeavored to see the "behavioral problems" his boss had raised as new challenges to be conquered. And he strove to patiently wait for the right job and the right time to come.

But each day it got harder and harder.

For James, it was undeniable that the costs were mounting up. Although he found the work easy, he enjoyed it less and less and consequently, mistakes were starting to crop up. In addition, his relationships with his peers and his team were strained as a result of his mood swings and his confidence was dented from the roles he'd lost. James' friends were concerned that whenever they saw him, all he did was moan about work. This was not what James wanted at all; he felt like he was going backwards not forwards.

Why does achievement matter in our jobs

James' desire for significant accomplishment, mastering of new skills and the need for progress was being thwarted by his boss' demands to stay in his current role. He felt like his efforts resulted in no real achievement towards his personal goal. Consequently, he was losing motivation, confidence and the ability to perform at his best. James was also worried that maybe he was becoming depressed.

If I've learnt anything by now it's that changing the way we perceive ourselves can dramatically improve our feelings and results. This was brought home to me for James when I met the extraordinary Stanford psychologist, Carol Dweck. A driven achiever and self-confessed perfectionist, Carol has made an art form out of studying people's mindsets and demonstrating how two beliefs in particular can make a difference.

People with a "fixed mindset" believe they're born with all the natural abilities they'll ever have and there is little that can be done to improve upon this. As a result, they tend to create performance goals – like being a successful businessman – because they believe that potential is measured by the validation received from others. When we believe that our abilities are basically static because they reflect the way that we're wired, then not surprisingly, we're more likely to avoid challenges, be unwilling to be seen to be exerting too much effort and feel threatened by negative feedback, because we fear that others will see any failures as an indication of all we lack. Unfortunately, both success and failure cause anxiety for people with this mindset. Failure, in particular, induces a state of helplessness, which means they don't pay attention to learning information, disengage from the problem and become depressed, de-energized and lose self-esteem when they inevitably give up.[1]

On the other hand, people with a "growth mindset" believe they're born with the capacity to improve their abilities through learning and effort. As a result, they tend to create learning goals around mastery and competence. When we believe that our abilities are like muscles that can be built up with practice, we are more willing to accept challenges, to put in our best effort and to accept criticism, because we understand that learning is the only way to keep getting better.

Creating goals for learning has been shown to increase our performance and enjoyment and decrease negative emotions. Failure and setbacks induce a response of mastery for people with a growth mindset that pushes them to focus on what they're learning, rather than how they feel, and galvanizes them to find new ways of doing things. And they are also then able to think "outside of the box" to solve problems because they believe they can.[2]

Carol explained to me that more important than believing in our own abilities is the mindset that we can improve these abilities. James was clearly struggling with his "fixed mindset". His sense of worth was so tied to reaching his goal of being a great business leader that although he had tried to keep making an effort and applying for new roles, he'd become dispirited and disheartened. By helping James to tune into the stories that he was telling himself and reframing these setbacks as learning opportunities, rather than failures that damn him to misery, he was able to move his mindset from fixed to growth. And by changing the way he perceived himself, James was able to start thinking more about learning goals, lighten his grip on his performance fixation and allow a glimmer of hope for new outcomes.

As I listened to James' story unfold, I couldn't help but also wonder what was driving his boss. Honestly, the guy sounded nice enough, but his reluctance to support James' growth and his fixation on James' "problems" indicated that something unfavorable was going on. His superior sounded like a Mixed Bag Boss – supportive one day and obstructive the next. After sharing his frustration with a peer, James found that his experience wasn't unique.

Mixed-Bag Bosses often swing from good to bad, because guilt governs their emotional life. Consumed by the idea that they've done a bad thing, or failed to do a good thing, they set about trying to make amends. For example, if his boss felt guilty for having impeded James' career progress, then he'd try to make it up to him in other ways like offering him a small pay rise (which James had just received) and providing training opportunities (which James would commence shortly) or the like.

On the one hand, James was flattered to think that his boss didn't want him to leave, but he knew he still had to find a way to get away from this guy. So, I asked, "Given the miracle you want and the understanding of what might be driving your boss, can you try to come up with at least six ways to complete the sentence: 'To improve the sense of accomplishment in my job by five per cent I could ...'." Here are some of the ideas we talked about, below.

OPTION 1: Rekindle hope

As we've established, what mattered most to James was the sense of accomplishment – that winning feeling – that would distinguish him as someone who counted. It was his greatest hope to embark on an exciting, challenging new role within the retailing giant to help him become a highly respected, successful business executive and for his boss to wish him all the best.

Hopes like these allow us to think positively and realistically about our future. When we're able to be clear about what we're hoping for (our goals), our ability to make it happen (our motivations) and the steps we should take (our pathways) then we're more likely to accomplish what we long for, even in the face of setbacks and challenges.[3]

While James was clear about his overall goal, it seemed he had run out of motivation and found himself on a pathway to nowhere. Perhaps the problem was that his goal wasn't very specific. What type of business role did he want and in what part of the organization? And what else could he do to progress towards this regardless of his boss?

Being as specific as possible is the first step in setting effective goals. "Be a respected business strategy expert" is a better goal than "be important" because it gives us a clear idea of what success looks like. Knowing exactly what we want to achieve helps to keep us motivated until we get there and assists us in identifying the specific actions or pathways to reach our goal.[4]

For example, given James' experience in designing business processes, understanding technological requirements and managing change, he could decide to become an expert in gamification – a new, emerging business trend. Gamification is the concept of applying online game mechanics to training investments, business processes and brand initiatives to make them more engaging. It's something areas like fashion retailing were already exploring and James could choose to be one of Australia's leading business gamification experts as a means of reaching his desire for accomplishment and importance. Now, that's a specific dream.

Once a goal has been set, it's important we shrink the change into smaller, manageable, concrete steps, which build our confidence, give us a sense of progress and keep us committed to the task at hand. Don't worry about a pathway requiring time, effort and persistence, because apparently the more difficult it looks the more likely we are to achieve our goal. As we start to plan out the steps, it's also worth thinking about which aspects of our goal we have control over and which we don't, so that we can identify the areas where our efforts will have the most impact and let go of those that won't – like changing our bosses.[5]

The pathway James had pursued to date was to apply for any business leader roles that came up, ranging from improving customer service to planning new retail outlets. Because his original goal had been so broad, he'd found it difficult to shrink the change into small, manageable steps other than just trying to get the roles – many of which he arguably wasn't qualified for.

If James' goal was more specific – like becoming one of Australia's leading business gamification experts – suddenly, additional pathways open up. He could certainly continue applying for any jobs inside the retailer looking for a business leader who can apply gamification knowledge, but there is also an array of small, concrete steps that he can take – none of which depend on his boss.

For example, James could join gamification groups to start building his networks; he could research blogs, publications, case studies, forecasts, conferences, and courses to improve his knowledge; and he could look for legitimate projects within his current role to build his gamification expertise. Almost all of this is within his control and would give him a sense of progress towards his goal.

Now that we know where we're going, all we have to do is seize the moment by deciding on actions for where, when and how. Again, it pays to be as specific as possible and "if/then" statements are a proven way to enhance our success by helping our brains to detect and seize opportunities to act. In fact, they improve our chances of success by roughly 300 per cent.[6] For example, if James sits down for lunch each day, then he will read a gamification blog.

And finally, it is very important that we keep a close eye on how far we have left to go. Achieving any goal requires honest and regular monitoring of our progress. Only by monitoring our progress – weekly or even daily, depending on the goal – can we be accountable for what we're achieving and what we still have to go.[7] It also gives us an opportunity to celebrate our achievements, which triggers the brain's reward system by inducing neurotransmitters such as dopamine (leaving us feeling energized, excited, happy and confident) and consolidates the neural connections on which mastery relies.[8]

People who set goals are more likely to succeed than those who do not. They also increase their levels of well-being and vitality because they: have a sense of purpose, believe they have some control, boost their self-confidence, draw on their relationships and feel fully engaged.[9] This can be an exercise you take on yourself or something that you share with your boss.

What specifically are you hoping for? What small, manageable steps will shape your pathway to success? Are you ready to seize every opportunity you get? How are you measuring and celebrating your progress?

OPTION 2: Manage your weaknesses

James' boss had identified areas of his behavior – particularly with his peers – that were being used as a reason to hold him back. Although he didn't agree with most of this feedback, James had tried to take it on board and find ways to fix his weaknesses.

It's common for bosses to want their employees to overcome weaknesses, but it can be a futile ordeal, both professionally and personally. This is because our weaknesses represent non-existent or underdeveloped neural pathways making it difficult to perform or replicate the desired behavior.[10] Of course, we now understand that this can be changed, but it literally requires us to rewire our brains through deliberate effort and repeated practice, with the estimates for mastery currently standing at around 10,000 hours.[11]

James found it tedious and exhausting to constantly monitor his behavior in meetings. Conscious of over-contributing, he tried to behave with prudence and humility so that others had a chance to innovate and take the lead, but constantly trying to fix these weaknesses rendered him disengaged, uninspired and dejected. He also felt fake and useless.

Managing our weaknesses is hard work. In contrast, building our strengths – like the VIA character strengths we read about in Chapter 5 – while still requiring effort, is more engaging, enjoyable and rewarding because achievements accrue far quicker. Our strengths represent dominant or well-developed neural pathways for which the path to mastery is already well underway.[12]

Given a choice, James would much rather build on his strengths than fix his weaknesses and in my experience, he's not alone. This doesn't mean we never need to fix a weakness. But it does mean we should make an informed choice about managing our weaknesses directly or using our strengths to improve our chances of success. For example, James is very strong in social intelligence and could use this strength to balance his contributions with his peers, rather than trying to act with prudence or humility which are far lesser strengths for him.

When we build on our strengths and daily successes – instead of focusing on failures – we simply learn more. And, it is building on our strengths, not fixing our weaknesses, which offers disproportionate gains when it comes to realizing our accomplishments.[13]

How can you use your strengths to manage your weaknesses and accelerate your progress towards the outcomes you most want to achieve?

OPTION 3: Get playful

James took his hope of becoming a successful and important business leader very seriously. It was one of his life-long goals. But being too serious can be bad for your career and worse for your general well-being.[14]

Despite the traditional management frowns that often come with the idea of having fun at work, the Harvard Business Review reports that executives with a sense of humor climb the corporate ladder more quickly and earn more money than their counterparts. In another survey of more than 700 CEOs of major organizations, a staggering 98 per cent said that they would hire a person with a good sense of humor over one who seemed to lack a sense of levity.[15]

The old-school view that play was a diversion from work is gradually being overthrown as scientists discover that enjoying our work – being engaged and emotionally involved – positively impacts our confidence, creativity, collaboration and productivity. Play has also proven to be a substantial force in how we think, feel, and learn. Consequently, workers who play and are viewed as emotionally involved in their jobs are more likely to be evaluated well by their bosses, as well as their co-workers.[16]

James is naturally quite a playful person, but his hunger to get to the top had seen him overlook this strength as one of his best means of getting ahead. But exactly how could he become more playful at work without jeopardizing his reputation?

One option, gaining popularity among executives in large organizations, is to turn work into a game – be it based in reality or online. By breaking our goals into small missions, setting a limited time frame, leveraging our strengths to overcome the obstacles and developing a meaningful way of keeping score, we're able to turn something overwhelming or tedious into something surprisingly motivating by making it fun and playful.[17]

For example, James could take his dream of embarking on an exciting, new role within the retailer that satisfied his need for accomplishment and turn it into the game of Job Hunt. He could determine the small wins he'd need to win the game – like updating his CV, finding upcoming vacancies, attending interviews, seeking feedback – and turn these into a series of missions to complete. He might then identify his top strengths and determine how these could be used to make the missions more successful and enjoyable. He could also accumulate hunting scores based on his effort, which could be traded for real-world incentives like attending the talk of a visionary business leader or sessions with a career coach. And he could then set himself a time goal of six months, at which time he will have either won the game or need to reconsider his goal.

It's hard to overstate how much easier it is to love what you previously hated when you turn a tough task into a game. Today, there is a growing array of smart phone applications (e.g. Embracing Change) and online games (e.g. Mindbloom), which can help us play with the sense of accomplishment that many of us crave in our jobs, but miss from our bad bosses.

Could turning your goals into a game unleash the benefits of play and boost your sense of progress and accomplishment?

OPTION 4: Turn failure into success

Part of the reason that James was finding it so hard to remain hopeful was the creeping suspicion that maybe he was a failure – can you hear his fixed mindset creeping in? Perhaps he wasn't advancing to the top because he didn't really have what it takes and his boss was actually right about his behaviors? As he applied for job after job and was knocked back, his nagging fear that he wasn't good enough was starting to paralyze his confidence.

To remain employable, let alone competitive, we must constantly learn and grow, and to learn and grow, we must fail. It is no coincidence that some of the most successful people throughout history – Abraham Lincoln, Albert Einstein, Thomas Edison, Henry Ford, The Beatles, and Michael Jordon – are the ones who have failed the most. Those who understand that failure is inextricably linked with achievement are the ones who learn, grow and ultimately do well. Their brains literally become smarter as a result. They learn to fail, or they fail to learn.[18]

Fixed mindsets aren't just set overnight. This is a pattern of thinking that is well-entrenched and it takes vigilance, effort and time to turn our beliefs into growth mindsets. The first step is to be aware of the stories that these mindsets trigger so that we can start to recognize their effect. By the way, some people are very growth mindset at home, but fixed mindset at work, so it pays to notice your patterns of thinking.

Once we're aware of this, we need to recognize that we have a choice in how we interpret challenges, setbacks and criticisms. We can interpret them as signs that our fixed talents or abilities are lacking, or we can interpret them as signs that we need to ramp up our strategies and effort, stretch ourselves and expand our abilities. If we choose the latter, then as we approach challenges we need to talk to ourselves in a growth mindset voice which encourages us to embrace the opportunity to learn, rather than only focus on outcomes.[19]

For example, James might take 15 minutes to write down how he is failing in his quest for the next role. He could describe what he's been doing, the thoughts he's been having and how he felt as he heard the rejections and how he feels now writing about them. He can challenge himself about what each failure is teaching him and any other benefits that may be emerging. If he repeats this exercise two or three additional times, not just about his current job search, but other challenges that he may have faced, James will reinforce that belief that failures can be his best opportunities to learn and begin to embrace a growth mindset. Samuel Beckett, once said: "Ever tried. Ever failed. No matter. Try again. Fail again. Fail better."[20] If we take on challenges wholeheartedly and learn from our setbacks and try again, then how we hear the criticism and act on it is in our hands.

Would re-framing your failures into learning opportunities improve your sense of progress so that you can open yourself up to even greater accomplishments?

OPTION 5: Tell your boss

Finally, there is always the option of verbally slapping your boss to wake them up to what you need. But remember to be clear about your intention and the outcome you wish you achieve.

A Mixed Bag Boss like James' has a fear of harming others so if this conversation incites their sense of guilt about doing the wrong thing, it's possible that they'll then go out of their way to put it right. For example, if James sought out this conversation he could say something like: "With the greatest respect, I feel like I'm being held back in my current role and to keep functioning at my best for you and the company I'd really appreciate it if we could please agree on a clear plan about when you'll support me advancing to my next role and how you would be willing to support my efforts."

If James just told his boss he was being held back, his superior may not know the best way to alleviate any guilt that he felt by striving to make it up to James. Over the next few days, he may go out of his way to be nicer to James, but that's unlikely to result in any real progress. By asking for what he needs from his boss – "when you'll support me advancing," and "how you would be willing to support my efforts" – James is providing clear opportunities for his boss to put the situation right. And, by offering something back – "so that in the meantime I can keep functioning at my best" – James is hoping to trigger his boss' automatic reciprocity reflex.[21]

Most importantly, the whole conversation is designed to trigger progress of some kind for James. Can you hold a positive, respectful conversation with your boss in which you tell them how you're feeling and ask for their help to accomplish what you need?

Are you ready to accomplish what you want?

James felt ready to try the sentence stem completion exercise once more: "To improve the sense of accomplishment in my job by five per cent I could...".

- Find another job with a boss who will allow me to be as successful as I'm capable of being.

- Be more specific about my hopes for success so that I can uncover other pathways to achieving what I want.

- Stop focusing on my weaknesses and work on building my strengths so that I feel like I'm achieving more.

- Turn my job hunt into a game to make the process more enjoyable and to see my progress improving by the day.

- Re-frame my failures as learning opportunities so that I find ways to grow from these experiences – even if they're not the ones I'd have personally chosen.

- Tell my boss respectfully that I feel I'm being held back and ask for ways he'd be willing to help me progress my efforts to find my next role so that I can continue performing at my best.

When he was done, I asked James to go over the responses and identify the ones which made sense to him, any he wanted to explore further and to remove the ones that were irrelevant. Once this was done, he decided that he'd try to get more specific about his hopes so he could find pathways around his boss. In addition, he resolved to focus more on his strengths to accomplish it.

James' plans are still underway. His boss moved on and although he's had a direct conversation with his next boss about how he was feeling and they agreed a path for progress, six months on nothing has eventuated and he's found himself becoming even more depressed.

Lately however, James has decided to focus on his passions outside of work to secure an unpaid internship or a new job that would progress him towards the type of achievements he now wants. With new hopes to light his path forward, he is feeling more positive, energized and confident. And he's found that all the failings of the past year have been good lessons in helping him to hone his approach. It's clear that some pathways of progress loop around rather than moving in a straight line and that the courage to undertake the journey – not just achieve the outcome – can be its own accomplishment.

REASON 5: You're not making any progress

Given the miracle you want and the understanding of what might be driving your boss, can you try to come up with at least six ways to complete the sentence: "To improve the sense of accomplishment in my job by five per cent I could...". Below, you'll find some of the questions to help guide you.

1. When it comes to what you want to accomplish at work, what are you hoping for specifically? What small, manageable steps will shape your pathway to success? Are you ready to seize every opportunity you get? How are you measuring and celebrating your progress?

2. How can you use your strengths to manage your weaknesses and accelerate your progress towards the outcomes you most want to achieve?

3. Could turning your goals into a game unleash the benefits of play and boost your sense of progress?

4. Would re-framing your failures into learning opportunities improve your sense of progress so that you can open yourself up to even greater accomplishments?

5. Can you hold a positive, respectful conversation in which you respectfully tell your boss how you're feeling and ask for their help to accomplish what you need?

When you're done, go over the responses and identify the ones which make sense to you, any you want to explore further and remove the ones that are irrelevant. Is there an idea left, or a combination of several, that you could use to overcome your bad boss?

If not, try the same exercise tomorrow and the day after that and be sure to ask people you trust for some help until you have an answer that gives you hope again.

Section C:
Finding win-win outcomes

Chapter Nine

How will you know you've won?

Despite our best intentions, building positive habits can be hard work, which is why 80 per cent of New Year's resolutions get broken every year.[1] Why? Because we think we can go from 0 to 60 in an instant, building ingrained life habits through the sheer force of willpower. In the words of William James, the father of modern psychology: "All our life, so far as it has definite form, is but a mass of habits – practical, emotional and intellectual – systematically organized for our weal or woe, and bearing us irresistibly toward our destiny, whatever the latter may be."[2]

Now, we're at the business end: this chapter looks at how to hold onto the positive habits you've started to build and exact the ultimate revenge – your lasting happiness – regardless of your boss.

Case study 9

"I have to tell you that in six years, this is the closest I've ever been to quitting," I told my last boss, my voice flooded with anger and frustration.

She tried to calm me down with platitudes about the market being tough everywhere, which was technically true, but I was fed up with working for bosses who treated people carelessly. To be fair, this boss was a lovely person. She was smart, kind, well-trained in leadership and extremely self-aware – to the point where she'd laughingly acknowledge her inability to stay focused on details that she found boring or irrelevant.

However, when she was fully engaged, there was no one I'd prefer to work for, but the problems came when the mundane details of my employment needed her attention.

Consequently, I'd had my hours halved at a moment's notice, disappointing pay rises texted to me after meetings, responsibilities added to my job, despite explicitly stating that I felt it compromised my integrity, and now an unprovoked email full of misunderstandings and abuse for my efforts sent to the CEO of the firm.

Had this happened several years ago, I'd have been cursing my boss, rallying against her perceived short-comings and working myself into a right state of negativity and helplessness. Luckily, since then, with the help of my studies and friends' wisdom, I'd learnt a few tricks that ensured I could handle this behavior more constructively. Here are the final secrets I discovered to making miracles happen when it comes to our bosses.

Will boredom nibble away at your victory?

I knew it was going to be a bumpy year when, days before I was due to return from maternity leave, my new boss called me and asked that instead of returning full-time – as I was legally entitled to do – that I come back on a "slow burn" to help ease her budgetary pressures. "What exactly is a slow burn?" I asked. Apparently, it was about two days a week.

Was she kidding?! I had a family to feed; childcare all organized. There was no way we could survive on a two-days-a-week salary. My "ticker-tape belief" of "not good enough" was ringing alarm bells as fear swept through me that I was no longer wanted by the firm. It was a perfect storm of negativity.

So, I took a long, slow breath and tried to remember all I'd learnt. Firstly, I took my "not good enough" fear and physically imagined putting it in my back pocket where it couldn't interfere for the moment.

Secondly, I tried to get myself into a more positive frame of mind by imagining the miracles that were possible now that more flexible employment was suddenly being offered.

Thirdly, I tried to guess what might be driving her behavior and concluded that it was likely she had a "ticker-tape belief" about loss, which is why she was renowned for being a Laissez-Faire Boss who disappeared whenever details pulled her down.

Finally, I went to my boss with respect and a shared goal to balance her budget, which would also leave me enthused for my role, and asked her for what I needed to make part-time employment work. She readily agreed.

Initially, I was ecstatic. I'd be working less, earning more and doing things I thought I liked better. Yet less than two months later, I felt no happier than before I'd negotiated my miracle. What had happened?

Unfortunately, the diminishing power of good things in our life is not uncommon, as I found out when I finally got to meet Professor Ed Diener from the University of Illinois. Ed is sometimes nicknamed "Dr. Happy", not just for his delightful personality, but for his 25 years of research on the measurement of well-being.

He explained that one of the patterns that repeatedly appears in his reviews of happiness is the presence of "hedonic adaptation", when what was once thrilling becomes no more than mildly pleasant. Interestingly, many lottery winners are no happier less than a year after their dreams of winning come true because of this phenomenon.[3]

Ed explained that, with the exception of a few potent events that temporarily raise and lower happiness, we tend to be relatively even-keeled where happiness is concerned. Tough times bring us down and joyous occasions are uplifting, but we quickly adapt to both. The problem is that pay rises, promotions and new jobs can all seem exciting and rewarding at first, but over time we adjust and their emotional luster dims.[4] So, while my new circumstances had provided a boost in positivity as I headed back to work, this had quickly worn off.

Ed reminded me, however, that with a sustained effort to modify the way I was thinking and behaving, it was possible to improve my happiness at work. So, I started making sure that each day I walked out of the office at lunch time, sat along the river and listened to music I loved to give me a jolt of joy. I threw myself into learning new things by watching video talks and reading the latest texts whenever I found rumination about my boss' flaws dragging me down. And I tried to make Tuesdays a day of kindness when I'd do at least five things to consciously help or appreciate others.

What efforts will you sustain to ensure adaptation doesn't eat away at your happiness at work?

Can you make your nervous system your ally?

The trick to maintaining my positivity no matter what happened at work lay in building positive habits that would guide me – rather than govern me. The problem with this approach, is that social psychologists have discovered that we each have a limited supply of willpower – the more we use it, the more it wears out – making new habits difficult to sustain.

The good news is they've also found that willpower can be strengthened with regular practice – just like a muscle – and reset with some simple tactics. For example, when you feel your resolve flagging and the excuses mounting, you can give your willpower a boost by replenishing glucose in the bloodstream with a spoonful of sugar or inducing positive emotions such as humor. In the long-term however, the best solution is to strengthen your reserves of willpower. Research shows that you can achieve this gradually by practicing daily exercises in self-control, such as improving your posture, altering verbal behavior, or using your non-dominant hand for simple tasks.[5]

Another technique I've discovered to build successful habits draws on James' advice 100 years ago to "make our nervous systems our ally". Neuroscientists have only recently proven the wisdom of this insight by identifying how exciting the neurons in our head causes them to fire and wire together into stronger neural pathways which improve the ease, speed and quality of regularly repeated behaviors.[6] I've found that in just 11 minutes of regular daily practice I can cement new habits into my brain by lowering the amount of energy it takes to get started, immersing myself in the desired behavior and celebrating what I've achieved.

I've found the hardest part of building habits is the amount of energy it takes to begin. This is because we need to excite the neurons in our brain so that they'll start firing and wiring together and neural pathways can take shape.[7] So, I reduce the amount of activation energy it takes to get started – even by just 30 seconds – and I quickly find myself in the midst of the behavior I desire.

For example, when I want to make sure I stop and walk outside for lunch, I set my iPhone alarm for noon and place it on the other side of the room next to my bag so that I'll have to get up and turn it off. Or, when I want to stop ruminating on things that upset me at work I program an action trigger in my mind like: "When I feel upset, then I will learn something new by reading a blog." To build my habit of kind acts, I anchored the behavior to things I already do like making a thank you the first email I send after turning on my computer.

Once I've begun, I try to spend a reasonable amount of time practicing the desired behavior so that I give the neurons time to wire together into well-formed neural pathways. The stronger these pathways, the easier and quicker the behavior becomes to repeat.[8] While it's easy to convince myself that there's never enough time in a day, I found that if I just practiced for even ten minutes I could get results. Thinking that I only needed ten minutes to read, or ten minutes to sit outside and listen to some music, was something I could manage even on the busiest days.

Finally, I try to never forget that our brains like novelty – it's one of the things that triggers dopamine, the happy neurotransmitter in our heads.[9] By varying the songs I listened to, the things I read and my kind acts, I was able to maintain enough variety among these activities to ensure I didn't adapt to them and become bored. And when occasionally the thought of reading another book didn't thrill me, I'd give myself a day off until I found the next author who excited me. Of course, the best way to protect against adaptation is to practice living mindfully and ensure that you're building habits, which guide, but never govern you.[10]

How are you building habits to ensure your well-being regardless of your boss?

Are you monitoring your progress?

For a while, things settled down and work was reasonably enjoyable. My boss still went missing in action whenever details got the better of her or decisions she didn't want to have to make were required, but I was getting better and better at reframing these occurrences to be about her "fear of loss", rather than my "not being good enough" beliefs. I can't begin to explain the relief – this enabled me to remain peaceful and present in our relationship instead of building up resentment and hostility. Then, it came time for the New Year budgets and to re-negotiate my salary.

Once I figured out what this next miracle looked like, we started several rounds of challenging, but honest conversations, about what we needed and what happy numbers looked like from where we each stood. They were the conversations we both needed to have and I was grateful for her transparency and persistence throughout. But in our final chat, although we spoke for an hour about a broad range of topics, the final amount was never brought up and before I knew it, my boss' next meeting arrived and I was waved off. A few hours later, her text came through with a number significantly below what I had asked for and an apology that her phone battery was about to go flat. How convenient. After that, the matter was never again discussed.

Of course, I could have made a fuss, but it was unlikely anything I tried would change the number once it was set (hmm, a story of helplessness or realism?). So, I decided that the most productive use of my energy was to find a way to live with it. But even with my best intentions and practices as I hauled myself to work over the coming weeks, negativity washed over almost every step. How had I come so far only to end up miserable once more?

Another thing Ed reminded me of, was that happiness shouldn't be looked at as just a destination I'm trying to reach, but as a way that I'm learning to live. Consequently, if we enjoy the activities required to work towards our goals, rather than just the occasional short-term highs from obtaining results, then the experience becomes more rewarding regardless of our results.[11] As Shakespeare said: "Things won are done; joy's soul lies in the doing."

The challenge I found in understanding that happiness is a process, and not a place, was measuring my progress. I knew that without effort, grit and a clear focus on my purpose, the positivity I had worked so hard to cultivate risked slipping away in the face of escalating negative experiences (remember Barb's positivity ratio of 3 to 1).

In Chapter 8 we learnt about the importance of honest and regular monitoring of our progress. By ticking a list, assigning points for our efforts or counting our small successes we're able to see the impact we're having. Accountability also allows us to face the truth about any gaps between our intentions and our actual behavior so that we can adjust our efforts when required.[12]

It's also important to celebrate our progress either by savoring or sharing our success. When we consciously take in our surroundings and experience our emotions with a powerful sense of appreciation for what's happening in that moment, we trigger our brain's reward system. [13]

In addition, sharing our successes with people who are genuinely interested in us also amplifies our happiness, boosts our self-esteem and enhances our relationships.[14] Not only does savoring and sharing make us feel good, but they help to consolidate the neural connections on which building positive habits rely.

When I started counting all the moments of positivity I was accumulating each day, it shifted my focus away from what was going wrong in my work, to what was going right. Although I remained unimpressed at my boss' skills of communication, I was able to regain my sense of happiness about my job.

How are you measuring and celebrating your progress, so that your journey becomes its own reward?

Is happiness the best revenge?

Back on track, I managed to pass the next few months in a state of reasonable happiness. My jolts of joy, rumination distractions and acts of kindness enabled me to sail through the choppy waters that encompass many large workplaces. And although my boss' communication continued to be haphazard I was able to reframe it within moments of these incidences to avoid triggering my "not good enough" beliefs and feel compassionate for her "fear of loss" and the many pressures she faced in her job. It disappointed me, but didn't upset me.

Things came to a head however, when my boss asked me to negotiate a collaboration with a highly sought-after, international psychology leader to help move our people strategy forward. After the tarnishing of my personal reputation during months of protracted negotiations due to organizational budget cuts and my boss' indecisiveness, the enjoyment of my job was rapidly diminishing once more.

Then, to top it all off, a senior leader in the firm sent an unprovoked and scathing email in which he decried the inappropriate nature of my efforts to the CEO and several other leadership team members. The leader involved never tried to call me to ask about what was being negotiated and why. When I called him and dispelled his concerns, he never offered an apology for the unprofessional manner in which he raised his concerns. And neither my boss, nor any of the leadership team, ever said a word to discourage his behavior – for which he was renowned.

After succumbing, momentarily, to the "guilty" pleasures of fuming and cursing, I imagined invoking all types of revenge until in a moment of silence I heard a little voice inside my head say: "Ah, just tell them to go fuck themselves." Even now, it still makes me laugh.

You see, even for all I'd learnt, each of us still believes that we see the world directly, as it really is. We also believe that the facts as we see them are there for all to see, therefore others should agree with us. If they don't agree then it follows that they don't yet have all the facts or that they're blinded by their own interests or ideologies. This phenomenon, known as "naive realism" gives us a world full of good and evil upon which the angels and devils fight it out.[15]

The reality is that nature created all of us to sometimes commit selfish and short-sighted acts to ensure our survival. Unfortunately, our tendency is to rarely blame ourselves, but all too quickly see the bias, greed and duplicity of others. Our ever-judging minds give us constant flashes of approval and disapproval, along with the certainty that we are always on the side of the angels.[16]

Our willingness to judge others is a disease of the mind that leads to anger, torment and conflict as we pursue success, rather than happiness, in games of moral tit-for-tat that make us want to return favor for favor, insult for insult, tooth for tooth, and eye for eye. As a result, we enthusiastically pursue goals which will help us win prestige in zero-sum games that provide a burst of momentary pleasure at someone else's loss, but no real lasting happiness. [17]

In reality, most people are doing their best to lead a good life and those with serious problems usually deserve our compassion. I've come to realize that only by understanding and accepting our own biases can we overcome hypocrisy, self-righteousness and moralistic judgments. Yes, that email probably should never have been written, but maybe I should have guessed the senior leader involved would have concerns and alerted him much sooner to what was happening. Being honest about our own faults opens us up to seek out more win-win solutions which allow for growth and happiness on all sides.

With my anger slightly dissolved, I was motivated and clear-headed enough to spend the night re-imagining my miracle. And with my family's blessing and my friends' encouragement, several days later I gladly offered a win-win solution to my boss which eased her ongoing budget pressures, provided me with some financial stability and allowed me to resign gracefully to pursue work with people who treated others respectfully. The feeling of relief on all sides was enormous and I was able to leave without bitterness, regret, or resentfulness.

I wasn't sure how I'd replace my salary – it had been more money than I ever dreamed of being paid – but I was sure by now that working every day with people who made me miserable was never going to be worth the price. Ultimately, I decided to bank on the fact that being happy at work would increase my effectiveness and fuel my performance to help me make more money, achieve goals more easily, receive more promotions, enjoy better job security, receive better supervisor ratings, and avoid becoming burnt-out – subsequently, providing the best revenge of all. And so far, I am "happy" to report it's working out.

Could a win-win solution that provides you with lasting happiness be the best revenge of all against your boss?

Questions to ask about what to do next

Grab a pen and paper and reflect on your answers to these questions as you work out how to ensure your victory lasts. These are only intended as thought starters, so as you get the hang of asking questions that open up possibilities, feel free to add more.

STEP 4: Realize that the best revenge is lasting happiness

1. Even the joy of winning the lottery is prone to "hedonic adaptation", when what was once thrilling becomes no more than mildly pleasant. So, what other efforts will you undertake to sustain your well-being at work and ensure that adaptation doesn't eat away at your happiness?

2. William James counseled that: "All our life, so far as it has definite form, is but a mass of habits – practical, emotional and intellectual – systematically organized for our weal or woe, and bearing us irresistibly toward our destiny, whatever the latter may be." How are you building habits that will ensure your well-being regardless of your boss?

3. When we enjoy the activities required to work towards our goals, rather than just the occasional short-term highs from obtaining results, then the experience becomes more rewarding. How are you measuring and celebrating your progress, so that your journey becomes its own reward?

4. Research shows that people who are happy at work increase their effectiveness and fuel their performance to make more money, achieve goals easier, receive more promotions, enjoy better job security, receive better supervisor ratings and avoid becoming burnt out –as a result, providing the best revenge of all. Can you create a win-win solution that provides you with lasting happiness?

Chapter Ten

How can you convince your organization to act?

A bad boss can be the worst thing that ever happens to us, but it can also be an opportunity for us to experience great post-traumatic growth (PTG). We may be able to come out stronger and more grounded, know ourselves better and go on to do bigger and better things as a result. In the words of Nietzsche: "What does not kill me makes me stronger."[1] How will your story end?

It's also essential that we help educate organizational leaders about the costs of bad bosses so that their poor behavior is no longer tolerated. Studies show that even model employees turn "negative and unproductive if their bosses are rude or mean spirited," gossiping rather than working, stealing, backstabbing and taking longer breaks. Not only that, but abused employees are also three times less likely to make suggestions, or go out of their way to fix workplace problems.[2] If you are a leader, what can you do to protect your employees and your business from bad bosses?

The high cost of bullying

This morning, I woke up to a story in the newspaper describing how a travel agent store manager routinely belittled an employee, telling her that she was "useless", she "stinks" and saying that she deserved to wear a "boob apron" – an apron complete with plastic boobs stuck on the front – at a work event because she had underperformed. Outraged and distressed at what was occurring, the assistant store manager made a formal complaint to head office about their boss' behavior and in return was himself bullied for the next six months.

The boss involved boasted of "doing little things to annoy him" like having the heater pumped up, laughing loudly, and singing Bon Jovi. She told other staff that the assistant store manager was a self-centered jerk and that she disliked his "four-eyed face" and encouraged his clients to make complaints about him. Eventually, after raising further complaints, the assistant manager was accused of acting inappropriately at work, given a warning, and told he'd have to shift stores. He resigned instead and is currently suing the travel chain for bullying in the workplace.[3]

Unfortunately, this story is just one of the thousands of cases of people being badly treated by their bosses that I discovered when preparing this book.

There was the boss who would take away his employees' chairs if they hadn't made a sale and make them work standing up until they made one. Next, the "team building" exercise that involved making a colleague lie on the floor, holding his head and then pouring water over his nose and mouth from a gallon jug to teach people how to fight hard for they what they want.[4]

How about the legal secretary who was treated as if she was invisible with people refusing to acknowledge her existence?[5] Or the waitress who after a repeated campaign of physical and psychological bullying – including being called names, having fish sauce poured on her, and rat poison left in her handbag – took her own life.[6]

As the list of these horrendous stories has continued to grow in recent years and their effects on people's careers, relationships and health has been documented, Australia, Canada, the UK, Ireland, and Sweden have all introduced anti-bullying legislation and at least 17 states in America are currently considering this option. While these legal protections are welcome, I'm a big believer that prevention is better than the cure and so this book was written to encourage employees and their organizations to more actively guide bosses towards better behaviors in our workplaces.

It's natural to feel victimized when someone we perceive as powerful – like our boss – starts infringing upon our rights, yet new research suggests that we all have the capacity to also act heroically. Studies have shown that effective acts of heroism can be learned, encouraged and achieved by anyone at any point in their lives. All it takes is the choice to actively try and address injustice or create positive change despite the fear that we may fail.[7]

What I've discovered from all the wonderful researchers, psychologists and leaders featured throughout this book is that heroes are not born, they are made.

A bad boss is our call to adventure which shakes us out of life as we've known it and into another realm that presents friends to count on, adversaries to overcome and trials to be undergone so that we can emerge wiser and stronger.[8] To help us navigate this journey we've learnt how to:

1. **Get real about what we're telling ourselves.** Being honest about what we're putting up with, the stress and negativity it's creating, what it's costing us in terms of our career, our relationships and our health, along with the stories of "victims", "villains" and "helplessness" that we're using to comfort ourselves, helps us to recognize that the situation with our bad boss needs changing.

2. **Own our own stories so we're ready to act.** Heroes work out what they're fighting for (not against) and behave accordingly, they challenge their "ticker-tape beliefs" that impede their progress, they find the compassion to understand the beliefs that drive others and they can access their powers of empathy, optimism and confidence to improve their relationships.

3. **Connect with others to create win-win outcomes.** Every hero needs a sidekick, so we need to reach out to someone whom we can trust and share our stories with, so that we can break the grip of shame, multiply our resources and come up with at least six different ways to create a win-win plan that delivers the miracle we want.

4. **Realize that the best revenge is lasting happiness.** In order to bask in the glory of our win, we need to protect our well-being at work by building healthy habits and continuously measuring and celebrating our progress. If we're happy in our jobs, we're more likely to increase our effectiveness and fuel our performance so we can earn more money, achieve goals more easily, receive more promotions, enjoy better job security, receive better supervisor ratings and avoid becoming burnt-out, therefore, providing the best revenge.

There's no need to live our lives in chains, when the key to change is in our hands. Are you ready to be a hero and rescue yourself from your bad boss?

What if you've become really stuck?

If, for one reason or another, you're no longer working for your bad boss, but the scars linger on, damaging your confidence and joy for life, don't lose heart – it's still possible to be a hero and find a happy ending. On average, most of us put up with bad bosses for around 22 months before we act – allowing the uncertainty, unpredictability, ambiguity, lack of personal recognition and the excessive physical and psychological demands to build into chronic stress.[9]

No wonder, new research has started to compare the symptoms displayed by people who have been in conflict situations, like soldiers, to workplaces where bullying occurs. Frighteningly, both groups have been found to suffer nightmares, are jumpy and seem fuelled by too much adrenaline. In addition, they show greater susceptibility to illnesses, heart disease and alcoholism. Overall, one in five people studied for workplace bullying exhibited the main symptoms of Post-Traumatic Stress Disorder (PTSD).[10]

While PTSD is most commonly associated with people who have suffered a single major life-threatening incident, such as wars, or natural disasters, there is a growing awareness among mental health professionals that similar injury can be caused as a result from an accumulation of many small, individually non-life-threatening incidents.

Known as Complex PTSD, it is caused by any prolonged period of negative stress which includes captivity, lack of means of escape, entrapment, repeated violation of boundaries, betrayal, rejection, bewilderment, confusion, and – crucially – lack of control, loss of control and disempowerment. Situations which might give rise to Complex PTSD include bullying, harassment, abuse, domestic violence, stalking, long-term caring for a disabled relative, unresolved grief, exam stress over a period of years, or mounting debts.[11]

Thought of as an injury, not an illness, Complex PTSD sufferers often experience:

1. Difficulties managing their emotions, depression and may have thoughts of suicide or feelings of extreme anger.

2. Repressed memories or flashbacks of their trauma.

3. Helplessness, shame, guilt or detachment that makes them withdraw from others.

4. Sleeplessness, nightmares and impaired concentration.

5. Anxiety or panic attacks when reminded of the experiences.

6. Physical and emotional numbness with an inability to feel joy.

7. The belief that they have no power over a perpetrator.

8. Problems in their personal relationships.

9. A loss of faith in humanity or feel overwhelmed by a sense of helplessness.[12]

Once diagnosed, the prospect of recovery is good when we have the right counsel and are in the company of fellow survivors and those with genuine insight, empathy and experience. If you suspect you may have Complex PTSD as a result of a bad boss, please take the first heroic step and ask a mental health professional for help.

Happily, it has also been discovered that reactions like Complex PTSD are not the only options when we've faced the kind of prolonged stress that can be caused by a bad boss. Studies have now found that there is also the chance of post-traumatic growth (PTG). It seems that a substantial number of people who show intense depression and anxiety after extreme adversity, often to the level of PTSD, arrive at a higher level of psychological functioning than before.[13]

When researchers studied people's responses to a variety of traumas: terminal illness, loss of a home in a natural disaster, divorce, military captivity, sexual assault, and having a low birth weight child, they found that a subset of individuals reported personal growth, strengthening, and even thriving because they had been forced to confront their personal priorities, sense of meaning, identity and purpose. Some of the common transformative experiences reported by such trauma survivors are as follows:

•   Renewed belief in their ability to endure and prevail.

•   Improved relationships – in particular, discovering who one's true friends are and whom one can really count on.

•   Feeling more comfortable with intimacy.

•   A greater sense of compassion for others who suffer.

•   Developing a deeper, more sophisticated and more satisfying philosophy of life.[14]

The studies on post-traumatic growth mean that no matter how the situation with your bad boss may have been resolved, there remains an opportunity for you to step forward and be your own hero so not only can you survive, not only can you recover, but you can flourish.

One proven mechanism of achieving this outcome is the disputation technique we learnt back in Chapter 2 to challenge the stories that we're telling ourselves and find new explanations. Another is finding meaning by writing – as expressively as possible – about our painful experiences over three to five days to help us understand, come to terms with and make sense of our trauma thereby reducing intrusive thoughts and lowering depression.

Finally, no matter how hard it may seem, it's important to never overlook the power of forgiveness. An act of kindness for yourself, rather than for your boss, is using your imagination to visualize what you could say and how you might feel to empathize with your boss and grant them forgiveness so that you can free yourself of resentment. Granting forgiveness doesn't imply excusing or tolerating your boss' behavior, but it does entail trying to let go of your hurt, anger, and hostility whilst adopting a more charitable perspective.[15]

Remember there is always a third path, which leads us from failure or setback to a place of learning and growth so that we're even stronger and more capable than before we fell. If you've become stuck after years of dealing with a bad boss, could treatment for Complex-PTSD or exercises for post-traumatic growth offer you a path to relief?

Why should companies welcome this conversation

The costs of having bad bosses quickly adds up for an organization – health care, lost productivity, theft, lost creativity, errors, recruiting and training costs, public relations expenses and legal costs – to name a few. And studies have shown that employees with abusive bosses are more likely than others to slow down or make errors on purpose (30 per cent Vs. 6 per cent), hide from their bosses (27 per cent Vs. 4 per cent), not put in maximum effort (33 per cent Vs. 9 per cent), and take sick time when they weren't sick (29 per cent Vs. 4 per cent).[16]

Abuse by a boss doesn't have to be extreme, researchers have found that even basic incivility and rudeness, such as the examples below, is enough to cause employees to deliberately decrease the quality of their work and negatively impact their performance.

- "My boss asked me to prepare an analysis. This was my first project, and I was not given any instructions or examples. He told me the assignment was crap."
- "My boss said: 'If I wanted to know what you thought, I'd ask you.'"
- "My boss saw me remove a paper clip from some documents and drop it in my wastebasket. In front of my 12 subordinates, he rebuked me for being wasteful and required me to retrieve it."
- "On speakerphone, in front of peers, my boss told me that I'd done 'kindergarten work.'"

And those who have been the targets of bad behavior are often, in turn, uncivil themselves: they sabotage their peers, they "forget" to copy colleagues on memos and they spread gossip to deflect attention. Faced with incivility, employees are likely to narrow their focus to avoid risks – and lose opportunities to learn in the process.[17]

It's clear that the bond between boss and employee is the prime predictor of both daily productivity and the length of time people stay at their jobs. Research shows that unhappy employees take more sick days, staying home an average of 1.25 more days per month, or 15 extra sick days a year.[18] In the US, it's estimated that companies lose $360 billion each year due to lost productivity from employees who have poor relationships with their supervisor.[19] In addition, more than 20 million Americans have left jobs to flee from workplace bullies, most of whom were bosses. [20]

At an individual level, one organization decided to deduct from a boss' salary the financial costs incurred by his bad behavior such as: anger management classes, legal fees to adjudicate complaints, time spent by senior management and HR professionals fretting over his misdeeds and the cost of hiring and training a series of people who worked under him. The total in one year? Some $160,000! It would have been cheaper to fire him.[21]

By now, smart companies have cottoned on to the fact that cultivating, recognizing and rewarding good bosses is good for business. For example, when the Gallup Research Organization asked ten million employees around the world if they could agree or disagree with the following statement: "My supervisor, or someone at work, seems to care about me as a person," those who agreed were found to be more productive, contributed more to profits, and were significantly more likely to stay with their company long-term. Other studies have found that employees with strong ties to their boss bring in more money than those with only weak ties – besting the company average by $588 of revenue each month.[22]

How can this be? Well, it seems the "glitter dust" of positivity is as powerful for teams as it is for each of us. During the 1990's a researcher by the name of Marcial Losada invited 60 different business teams to craft their business missions and strategic plans in a special laboratory that he created to look like an ordinary boardroom. It had the usual large table surrounded by executive-style chairs, but the walls sported one-way mirrors and behind these sat Losada's team of research assistants, equipped with video cameras and specially programmed computers.

They coded every single statement – large and small – made by every single team member during the hour-long business meetings into three dimensions: whether people's statements were (1) positive or negative, (2) self-focused or other-focused, and (3) based on inquiry (asking questions) or advocacy (defending a point of view). Losada also quantified how much each team member influenced the behavior of others and called this new variable the team's connectivity.

Determined to help business teams with poor performance records become more successful, Losada contrasted independent data on profitability, customer satisfaction ratings, and evaluations by superiors, peers, and subordinates with what he'd observed in the interactions. An extraordinary pattern started to emerge.

The organizations that rated "high" for business outcomes (about twenty-five per cent of those who participated) had unusually high positivity ratios (the ratio of positive statements to negative statements) at about 6 to 1, asked questions as much as they defended their own views and cast their attention outward as much as inward.

By contrast, the organizations which rated "low" for business outcomes (about thirty per cent) had positivity ratios well below 1 to 1, had far lower connectivity, asked almost no questions and showed almost no outward focus.[23] It seems that positivity in work environments broadens our minds, opens our hearts and builds the resources of business teams, just like it does for each of us individually.

Losada took his research one step further to discover that through simple algebra, in which the control parameter used was the connectivity he'd observed among team members, he could translate his findings into a positivity ratio which predicted business performance. According to Losada's math, the magic positivity ratio is 2.9013 to 1, or for those of us who are more practical, 3 to 1. Does this number sound familiar? That's right; it's the exact same ratio that Barb Fredrickson's research found as the tipping point for individual flourishing.[24]

Add to this the impact of workplace contagion and it becomes easy to see how the behavior of bosses can have such a powerful impact on organizational outcomes. In fact, our emotions are so shared, that organizational psychologists have found that each workplace develops its own group emotion, or "group affective tone," which over time creates shared "emotion norms" that are proliferated and reinforced by the behavior, both verbal and non-verbal, of the employees. So, badly behaved bosses not only lower their own positivity ratio, but they spread it right around the team, whereas kind, happy and respectful bosses boost the positivity ratio for themselves and the people around them.[25]

If you're the leader of an organization, are you being realistic about what bad bosses cost?

How can organizations help bosses do a better job?

There is no single or magical thing that defines a great boss. It seems the best bosses understand the power of a positive mindset and don't spread their emotional debris across the office. They also: understand our strengths and are interested in helping us find ways to use and develop them so that we're engaged in our work; foster good relationships that make us feel relaxed and comfortable, so that we can go about our jobs more efficiently; provide context for our roles and appreciate the need for purpose in the tasks assigned to us; and they give us the freedom to progress, being quick to praise a job well done, but also giving periodic feedback about opportunities for improvement.

Is this achievable? With all that positive psychology has uncovered over the last decade, the answer is absolutely yes. It's been my great pleasure in recent years to work with organizations that want to help their bosses become better leaders. They do this by teaching managers the skills to:

- **Boost their positivity** – In addition to all the options laid out in Chapter 4, simple interventions like starting meetings with "What's going well?" and taking the time to personally thank people for their efforts can shift the mood of a team. Other organizations take a more hands-on approach, like Google who is famous for keeping scooters in the hallway, video games in the break room and gourmet chefs in the cafeteria. Or Patagonia, who in addition to the "Let My People Go Surfing" policy whenever employees need a break, also regularly offers "brain-food" classes covering topics such as surfing, yoga, time management, introduction to French culture, etcetera. Why bother? If people are having fun, they're going to work harder, stay longer, maintain their composure in a crisis and take better care of the organization.[26]

- **Engage their strengths** – Marrying personal strengths to job requirements can reinvigorate an employee around their role and outcomes. You won't be surprised to learn that based on their research, Gallup has a company policy of focusing on employee strengths, which is why every employee has their strengths listed on their office door. But you may be interested to learn that organizations like Toyota's North American Parts Centre have seen an instant jump in productivity when it instituted strengths-based training for employees. Remember earlier we saw that compared to those who do not get to focus on what they do best, people who have the opportunity to use their strengths are six times as likely to be engaged in their jobs and more than three times as likely to report having an excellent quality of life.[27]

- **Cultivate good relationships** – Taking the time to respond actively and constructively to people's good news and investing in casual social opportunities during office hours helps people to feel safer within a team. For example, at San Francisco-based industrial design firm IDEO, teams are encouraged to take an afternoon off now and then and see a movie or a ball game. Or, at UPS, truck drivers are encouraged to stop and have lunch with three of four other drivers so that they can swap stories, information and misplaced packages and build friendships. Why? Because the organization has come to understand that this social interaction pays back in the long run, not just for the individual drivers, but for the company as a whole. Socially connected teams enjoy lower absenteeism and turnover rates and increased employee motivation and engagement.[28]

- **Encourage a sense of purpose** – Being clear about what gives us purpose and allows us to connect our efforts with something larger than ourselves allows people to move from jobs and careers to callings. This is why Chip Conley, CEO of a wildly successful chain of boutique hotels, tells employees: "Forget about your current job title. What would our customers call your job title if they described it by the impact you have on their lives?" And why companies like Harley-Davidson invite some 50 employees to help review grants and guide company giving. Calling-orientated workers are passionate about what they do and gain great happiness and satisfaction from their job enabling them to perform with greater dedication and better results.[29]

- **Recognize and celebrate accomplishment** – Understanding people's need for a sense of progress, so that feedback is immediate and often and celebration is prioritized, is essential to ensure that accomplishments – big and small – are not overlooked in our rush to get everything done. Simple, inexpensive rituals of recognition can ensure people feel valued and important. At Budget Rent A Car in Western Canada's corporate office employees vote on the happiest person each week and decorate the winner's desk with balloons and other prizes to boost morale. Or, how about the Walk-the-Talk Award created by a chairman who handed out a novelty store set of 39-cent chattering teeth whenever people lived the corporate values. It might seem like a silly prize, but when chattering teeth are proudly displayed on employees' desks, it's a good reminder that celebrations don't have to be expensive to be effective. Pleasure comes as much from making progress towards a goal, as it does from achieving them, so it's important to provide specific, deliberate and immediate recognition and rewards around big and small accomplishments. Done right, celebrating people's accomplishments can be even more motivating than money.[30]

Something interesting starts to happen when you improve a boss' level of well-being – it ripples outward. Teams that have a boss who is more positive and happy experience less group conflict, more cooperation and – most importantly – greater overall performance on the tasks at hand.[31]

Much can be added to these basic steps and there is a wealth of management literature on which to draw upon for inspiration, but the ideas detailed here are grounded purely in Marty's formula for well-being: positive emotion, engagement, relationships, meaning and accomplishment (or PERMA). During a recent chat about leadership, Marty noted to me that while teaching bosses the knowledge and skills of building PERMA was a worthy endeavor for organizations, he also believes that increasing well-being in teams is largely a local affair shaped by the beliefs and actions of individual leaders.

Marty's point is exactly why I believe smart organizations will not only welcome, but will encourage their employees to stand up for their rights; so that when their well-being is consistently and persistently compromised by the actions of a bad boss they should, with the greatest respect, tell their boss to go fuck themselves.

Given that the majority of bad bosses are good people doing a bad job, raising awareness of how their beliefs and behaviors are negatively impacting us is essential if they're to have the chance to use the skills organizations are giving them to learn and grow. Every boss is prone to bouts of cluelessness and to forgetting the effects that their position of power can have. They need support from the top-down in the form of company sponsored education and training and from the bottom-up in the form of courageous subordinate feedback if they are to improve their leadership competencies and reduce the risk of self-delusion.

Marty suggested if this is not enough to get bosses focused on the team's well-being and their excuses about lack of time, fear of undermining their authority and a perpetual crisis-mode mindset are hard to overcome, then organizations should also consider measuring team PERMA. When Boss A realizes that Boss B is outperforming them on team well-being, Boss A will find all sorts of imaginative ways to catch up.

"In the end though, Michelle," he said, "While leaders can be taught the skills of PERMA and employees can help improve a boss' level of self-awareness, the most effective strategy of all for an organization is to select bosses for their positivity and their ability to nurture well-being."

While some elements of this selection seem to occur naturally – the Harvard Business Review reports that executives with a sense of humor climb the corporate ladder more quickly[32] – it certainly doesn't occur consistently as the sheer number of people encountering bad bosses attests. Yet measuring positivity and well-being is a simple, non-invasive test which can be reliably performed in minutes and could easily be incorporated into any hiring or promotion process.

People don't quit organizations, they quit bad bosses.[33] Perhaps of even greater concern, however, is that before they quit 56 per cent of people with crummy bosses report that they are "checked-out" and "sleepwalking through their days", while the most bitter 18 per cent who are actively disengaged undermine their co-workers' accomplishments. However, in businesses where a higher proportion of employees report that their immediate bosses care about them – employee satisfaction, retention, and productivity are higher and so is profitability.[34]

If you're the leader of an organization, could well-being training, measurement and selection – as well as more honest upward feedback – save you millions of dollars in lost productivity, absenteeism and turnover?

Can we learn to get along?

Many of the stories that I uncovered about bad bosses while preparing this book were enough to bring me to tears. That bosses could be so unhappy, insecure, afraid and lacking in self-awareness to treat others in such thoughtless, mean and nasty ways is human nature at its very worst. But also that people could become so sad, ashamed and overwhelmed that they create stories of "victims", "villains", and "helplessness" to justify them doing nothing to improve their situations, or free themselves of their tormentors, drove me to despair.

It takes two people to create a bad relationship. But it takes just one person to start acting differently to change it. This doesn't mean we need to paint a fake smile on our face and pretend that things are okay when they're not, but it does mean that we can be realistic about the present, change our narrative about what we can do rather than what we can't and make small choices which begin to maximize our well-being for the future that we want. And we can remember to laugh along the way by reminding ourselves that we could always just tell our boss with the greatest respect to go fuck themselves.

In the words of one of my favorite positive psychology business researchers Shawn Achor: "Happiness is not the belief that we don't need to change; it is the realization that we can".[35]

Further Resources

What is workplace bullying?

Any behavior that is repeated, systematic, and directed towards an employee or group of employees can be considered workplace bullying, if a reasonable person would expect it to victimize, humiliate, undermine, or threaten. It places your health, well-being, safety and career at risk, interferes with job performance and creates a toxic working environment. Workplace bullying can attack anyone, in any career, at any level, within any organization, at any time.

What does bullying in the workplace look like?

- Repeated hurtful remarks or attacks, or making fun of your work or you as a person

- Yelling and shouting

- Sexual harassment, particularly behavior like unwelcome touching and sexually explicit comments and requests that make you feel uncomfortable

- Excluding you or stopping you from working with people or taking part in activities that relate to your work

- Playing mind games, ganging up on you, or other types of psychological harassment

- Intimidation (making you feel less important and undervalued)

- Giving you pointless tasks which have nothing to do with your job

- Allocating you impossible jobs that can't be done in the given time, or with the resources, provided including an unrealistic workload

- Deliberately changing your work hours or schedule to make it difficult for you

143

- Deliberately holding back information you need for getting your work done properly or micromanaging you

- Pushing, shoving, tripping, or grabbing you in the workplace

- Blackmail or sabotage of your career or financial status

- Spreading malicious rumors and gossiping about you

- Attacking or threatening with equipment, knives, guns, clubs or any other type of object that can be turned into a weapon.

- Initiation or hazing – where you are made to do humiliating or inappropriate things in order to be accepted as part of the team.

What you can do if you are being bullied at work

- Make sure you're informed. Check to see if your workplace has a bullying policy and complaints procedure.

- Keep a journal. Document everything that happens, including what you've done to try and stop it. This can help if you make a complaint.

- Get support from someone you trust or contact support services. Even if you don't know anyone you can talk to, there are support services which are immediately available to help and support you in the Get Help section. This includes contacting your union.

- Approach the bully. If you feel safe and confident, you can approach the person who is bullying you and tell them that their behavior is unwanted and not acceptable. If you are unsure how to approach them, you might be able to get advice from an appointed contact person, or from a colleague or manager.

- Tell someone at your work. Your workplace will usually have a process for making a complaint and resolving disputes, which might include a warning, requiring the bully to have counseling, a mediation process, or even firing the bully if the situation continues. The person to talk to might be your supervisor/manager, a harassment contact officer, or a health and safety representative (if your work has one).

- Get information and advice. If the bullying is serious, if the situation has not changed after complaining to your manager, or if there is not anyone you can safely talk to at work, you can get outside information and advice.

Getting help in the United States

Bullying in general is not illegal in the US unless it involves harassment based on race/color, creed (religion), national origin, sex, age (40+), disability, HIV/AIDS or Hepatitis C status. However, changes are underway with many states reviewing the Healthy Workplace Bill. In the meantime you can find more advice on dealing with bullying in the US at **http://www.workplacebullying.org/**.

Information printed with the kind permission of ReachOut.com. For more in Australia, visit **http://au.reachout.com/**.

Bibliography

Chapter One

[1] Sutton, Robert I. (2010). Good Boss, Bad Boss: How to Be the Best... and Learn from the Worst. New York, NY: Hachette Book Group.

[2, 5] Seligman, M.E.P (2011). Flourish: A Visionary New Understanding of Happiness and Well-being. New York, NY: Free Press.

[3] Ratey, J.J. (2008). Spark: The Revolutionary New Science of Exercise and the Brain. New York, NY: Hachette Book Group USA.

[4] Medina, J. (2008). Brain Rules: 12 Principles for Surviving and Thriving at Work, Home and School. Seattle, WA: Pear Press.

[6, 15] Fredrickson, B. (2009). Positivity: Groundbreaking Research Reveals How To Embrace The Hidden Strength of Positive Emotions, Overcome Negativity, and Thrive. New York, NY: Crown Publishers.

[7] Achor, S. (2010). The Happiness Advantage: The Seven Principles of Positive Psychology That Fuel Success and Performance at Work. New York, NY: Crown Publishing.

[8] (November 29, 2011) "Abusive Boss Puts Strain On Family Life." United Press International. Retrieved January 4, 2012 http://www.upi. com/ Health_News/2011/11/29/Abusive-boss-puts-strain-on-family-life/UPI-49681322548043/?spt=hs&or=hn.

[9] Rath, T. & Harter J. (2010). Well-being: The Five Essentials Elements. New York, NY: Gallup Press.

[10] Diener, E. & Bisaws-Diener, R. (2008). Happiness: Unlocking The Mysteries of Psychological Wealth. Malden, MA: Blackwell Publishing.

[11] Cooperrider, D.L., Sorensen, P.F., Yaegar, T.F. & Whitney, D. (2001) Appreciative Inquiry: An Emerging Direction for Organization Development. Champaign IL; Stipes Publishing L.L.C.

[12, 13] Reivich, K. & Shatte, A (2002). The Resilience Factor: 7 Keys to Finding Your Inner Strength and Overcoming Life's Hurdles. New York, NY: Broadway Books.

[14] Kashdan, Todd (2009). Curious? Discover the Missing Ingredient to a Fulfilling Life. New York, NY: HarperCollins.

[16] Gostick, A. & Christopher C. (2008). The Levity Effect: Why it Pays to Lighten Up. Hoboken, New Jersey: John Wiley & Sons Inc.

[17] Stephens, R. & Umland, C. (2011). Swearing as a response to pain – effect of daily swearing frequency. Journal of Pain, 12, 1274-1281.

Chapter Two

[1, 22, 23] Sutton, Robert I. (2010). Good Boss, Bad Boss: How to Be the Best...and Learn from the Worst. New York, NY: Hachette Book Group.

[2] Rath, T. & Harter J. (2010). Well-being: The Five Essentials Elements. New York, NY: Gallup Press.

[3] "If one thing could make your job better what would it be?" Retrieved December 20, 2012 from http://www.workrant.com.

[4] Brown, Jeff; Fenske, Mark (2010-03-25). The Winner's Brain: 8 Strategies Great Minds Use to Achieve Success (p. 69). Perseus Books Group. Kindle Edition.

[5] Metcalf, L. (2007). The Miracle Question: Answer It and Change Your Life. Carmarthen, UK: Crown House Publishing.

[6] Cooperrider, D.L. (2001). Positive Images, Positive Action: The Affirmative Basis of Organizing. In Cooperrider, D.L., Sorensen, P.F., Yaeger, T.F. & Whitney, D. (Eds), Appreciative Inquiry: An Emerging Direction for Organizational Development. Champaign, IL: Stipes Publishing.

[7, 26] Achor, S. (2010). The Happiness Advantage: The Seven Principles of Positive Psychology That Fuel Success and Performance at Work. New York, NY: Crown Publishing.

[8] Heath, Chip; Heath, Dan (2010). Switch: How to Change Things When Change Is Hard. New York, NY: Broadway Books.

[9] Lyubomirsky, S. (2008). The How Of Happiness: A Scientific Approach To Getting The Life You Want. New York, NY: The Penguin Press.

[10, 17] Reivich, K. & Shatte, A (2002). The Resilience Factor: 7 Keys to Finding Your Inner Strength and Overcoming Life's Hurdles. New York, NY: Broadway Books.

[11] Fredrickson, B. (2009). Positivity: Groundbreaking Research Reveals How You Embrace The Hidden Strength of Positive Emotions, Overcome Negativity, and Thrive. New York, NY: Crown Publishers.

[12, 13, 14, 15] Riggio, R.E. (February 11, 2011) "The Four Types Of Bosses We Hate" Psychology Today. Retrieved December 20, 2012 http:// www.psychologytoday.com/blog/cutting-edge-leadership/201102/ the-four-(Ftypes-bosses-we-hate.

[16] (July 5, 2011) "Nearly Half of Employees Said They Have Worked For Unreasonable Managers; One In Four Suffer Through Torment" Office Team Survey. Retrieved December 5, 2011 http://www.sys-con.com/node/1896731.

[18] Kashdan, Todd (2009). Curious? Discover the Missing Ingredient to a Fulfilling Life. New York, NY: HarperCollins.

[19] Baron-Cohen, S. (2011) The Science of Evil: On Empathy and The Origins of Cruelty. New York, NY; Basic Books.

[20] Milgram, Stanley (1963). "Behavioral Study of Obedience". Journal of Abnormal and Social Psychology 67 (4): 371–8.

[21] Zimbardo, P.G. (2007). The Lucifer Effect: Understanding How Good People Turn Evil. New York: Random House.

[24] Goleman, D. (2006) Social Intelligence. New York, NY: Bantam.

[25] Medina, J. (2010). Brain Rules For Baby: How To Raise A Smart and Happy Child from 0 to 5. Seattle, WA: Pear Press.

Chapter 3

[1] Brown, B. (2007). I Thought It Was Just Me (But It Isn't): Women Reclaiming

Power and Courage in a Culture of Shame. New York, NY:Gotham Books.

[2] Brown, B. (2010). The Gifts of Imperfection: Let Go of Who You Think You're Supposed to Be and Embrace Who You Are. Center City, Minnesota: Hazelden.

[3] Lyubomirsky, S. (2008). The How Of Happiness: A Scientific Approach To Getting The Life You Want. New York, NY: The Penguin Press.

[4,6,8] Achor, S. (2010). The Happiness Advantage: The Seven Principles of Positive Psychology That Fuel Success and Performance at Work. New York, NY: Crown Publishing.

[5] Gostick, A. & Christopher C. (2008). The Levity Effect: Why it Pays to Lighten Up. Hoboken, New Jersey: John Wiley & Sons Inc.

[7] Diener, E. & Biswas-Diener, R. (2008). Happiness: Unlocking The Mysteries of Psychological Wealth. Malden, MA: Blackwell Publishing.

[9] Branden, N. (1994) The Six Pillars of Self-Esteem: The Definitive Work On Self-Esteem By The Leading Pioneer In The Field. New York, NY: Bantam Books.

[10] Sheth, J,N. Sisodia, R,S. & Wolfe, D,B. (2007). Firms of Endearment: How World-Class Companies Profit from Passion and Purpose Upper Saddle River, New Jersey: Wharton School Publishing.

[11] Biswas-Deiner, R.. (2011). Positive Psychology As Social Change. New York, NY: Springer.

[12] Rath, T. & Harter J. (2010). Well-being: The Five Essentials Elements. New York, NY: Gallup Press.

Chapter Four

[1,7] Diener, E. & Bisaws-Diener, R. (2008). Happiness: Unlocking The Mysteries of Psychological Wealth. Malden, MA: Blackwell Publishing.

[2] Seligman, M.E.P. (2002). Authentic Happiness: Using the New Positive Psychology to Realize Your Potential for Lasting Fulfillment. New York, NY: Simon & Schuster

[3,4,6,8,11,14,18,19,23] Fredrickson, B. (2009). Positivity: Groundbreaking Research Reveals How To Embrace The Hidden Strength of Positive Emotions, Overcome Negativity, and Thrive. New York, NY: Crown Publishers.

[5] Achor, S. (2010). The Happiness Advantage: The Seven Principles of Positive Psychology That Fuel Success and Performance at Work. New York, NY: Crown Publishing.

[9] Miller, C.A. & Frisch, M.B. (2010). Creating Your Best Life: The Ultimate Life List Guide. New York, NY: Sterling.

[10] R. J., J. Kabat-Zinn, et al. (2003), "Alterations in brain and immune function produced by mindfulness meditation," Psychosomatic Medicine 65: 564–70.

[12] Ratey, J.J. (2008). Spark: The Revolutionary New Science of Exercise and the Brain. New York, NY: Hachette Book Group USA.

[13, 16, 20, 22] Lyubomirsky, S. (2008). The How Of Happiness: A Scientific Approach To Getting The Life You Want. New York, NY: The Penguin Press.

[15, 17] Seligman, M.E.P. (1990). Learned Optimism: How To Change Your Mind & Your Life. New York, NY: Simon & Schuster.

[16] Reivich, K. & Shatte, A (2002). The Resilience Factor: 7 Keys to Finding Your Inner Strength and Overcoming Life's Hurdles. New York, NY: Broadway Books.

[21] Seligman, M.E.P (2011). Flourish: A Visionary New Understanding of Happiness and Well-being. New York, NY: Free Press.

[24] Switzler, Al; McMillan, Ron; Grenny, Joseph (2011). Crucial Conversations Tools for Talking When Stakes Are High, Second Edition. New York, NY: McGraw-Hill.

Chapter 5

[1, 7] Rath, T.(2007). Strengths Finder 2.0. New York, NY: Gallup Press.

[2, 9] Cszentmihalyi, M (1991). Flow: The Psychology of Optimal Experiences. New York, NY: Harper Collins Publishers.

[3] Peterson, C. (2006). A Primer in Positive Psychology. New York, NY: Oxford Press.

[4] Miller, C.A. & Frisch, M.B. (2010). Creating Your Best Life: The Ultimate Life List Guide. New York, NY: Sterling.

[5, 10] Lyubomirsky, S. (2008). The How Of Happiness: A Scientific Approach To Getting The Life You Want. New York, NY: The Penguin Press.

[6] Seligman, M.E.P. (2002). Authentic Happiness: Using the New Positive Psychology to Realize Your Potential for Lasting Fulfillment. New York, NY: Simon & Schuster.

[8] Biswas-Deiner, R. (2010) Practicing Positive Psychology Coaching: Assessment, Activities and Strategies for Success. Hoboken, New Jersey: John Wiley & Sons Inc.

[11] Wrzesniewski, A., & Dutton, J.E. (2010). Crafting a job: Revisioning employees as active crafters of their work. Academy of Management Review 26(2), 179-201.

[12] (December 4, 2009): You're your Job? Here's How To Reshape It." Time Magazine. Retrieved on January 15, 2012 http://www.time. com/time/business/article/0,8599,1944101,00.html.

[13] Siegel, D.J. (2009-11-30). Mindsight: The New Science of Personal Transformation. New York, NY; Bantam.

[14, 15] Langer, Ellen J. (2007). On Becoming an Artist: Reinventing Yourself Through Mindful Creativity. New York, NY: Ballantine Books.

[16] Gostick, A. & Christopher C. (2008). The Levity Effect: Why it Pays to Lighten Up. Hoboken, New Jersey: John Wiley & Sons Inc.

Chapter 6

[1, 11] Rath, T. & Harter J. (2010). Well-being: The Five Essentials Elements. New York, NY: Gallup Press.

[2, 3] Vaillant, G. (July 16, 2009). Yes, I stand by my words, "Happiness equals love—full stop." Positive Psychology News Daily. Retrieved 12 February, 2012, from http://positivepsychologynews.com/news/ george-vaillant/200907163163.

[4] Vaillant, G.E. (2009). Spiritual Evolution: How We Are Wired For Faith, Hope and Love New York, NY: Broadway Books.

[5, 6, 7, 9, 14] Achor, S. (2010). The Happiness Advantage: The Seven Principles of Positive Psychology That Fuel Success and Performance at Work. New York, NY: Crown Publishing.

[8] Heaphy E., & Dutton, J. E. (2008). Positive social interactions and the human body at work: Linking organizations and physiology. Academy of Management Review, 33, 137–.

[10, 12, 13, 15, 16] Lyubomirsky, S. (2008). The How Of Happiness: A Scientific Approach To Getting The Life You Want. New York, NY: The Penguin Press.

[17] Goleman, D. (2006) Social Intelligence. New York, NY: Bantam.

Chapter 7

[1, 3, 7, 10] Ben Shahar, T. (2007). Happier: Learn the Secrets to Daily Joy and Lasting Fulfillment. New York, NY: McGraw Hill.

[2] Steger, M. F., & Dik, B. J. (2010). Work as meaning: Individual and organizational benefits of engaging in meaningful work. In P. A. Linley, S. Harrington, & N. Garcea (Eds.), Oxford Handbook of Positive Psychology and Work. Oxford University Press.

[4] Achor, S. (2010). The Happiness Advantage: The Seven Principles of Positive Psychology That Fuel Success and Performance at Work. New York, NY: Crown Publishing.

[5] Diener, E. & Bisaws-Diener, R. (2008). Happiness: Unlocking The Mysteries of Psychological Wealth. Malden, MA: Blackwell Publishing.

[6] Wrzesniewski, A. (2003). Finding positive meaning in work. In K. Cameron, J. Dutton, and R. Quinn (Eds.), Positive organizational scholarship: Foundations of a new discipline (pp. 296-308). San Francisco: Berrett-Kohler.

[8] Wrzesniewski, A., & Dutton, J.E. (2010). Crafting a job: Revisioning employees as active crafters of their work. Academy of Management Review 26(2), 179-201.

[9] Sheldon, K. M., and Elliot, A. J. (1999). Goal striving, need satisfaction, and longitudinal well-being: The self-concordance model. Journal of Personality and Social Psychology, 76: 546–57.

[11] Lyubomirsky, S. (2008). The How Of Happiness: A Scientific Approach To Getting The Life You Want. New York, NY: The Penguin Press.

[12] Algoe, S.B., Haidt, J., & Gable, S.L. (2008). Beyond reciprocity: Gratitude and relationships in everyday life. Emotion, 8, 425 – 429.

Chapter 8

[1,2,19] Dweck. C.(2008). Mindset: The New Psychology of Success. New York, NY: Ballantine Books.

[3] Snyder C.R. (2000). Handbook of Hope: Theories, Measures and Applications. San Diego, CA: Academic Press.

[4,6] Grant Halverston, H. (2011) Succeed: How We Can Reach Our Goals. New York, NY; Hudson Street Press.

[5] Achor, S. (2010). The Happiness Advantage: The Seven Principles of Positive Psychology That Fuel Success and Performance at Work. New York, NY: Crown Publishing.

[7] Loehr, J. & Schwartz,T. (2003). The Power Of Full Engagement: Managing Energy, Not Time, Is the Key to High Performance and Personal Renewal. New York, NY: The Free Press.

[8,10,12] Doidge, N. (2007) The Brain That Changes Itself: Tales of Personal Triumph from the Frontiers of Brain Science. New York, NY: Penguin.

[9] Lyubomirsky, S. (2008). The How Of Happiness: A Scientific Approach To Getting The Life You Want. New York, NY: The Penguin Press.

[11] Gladwell, M. (2009). Outliers: The Story of Success.

[13] Rath, T. (2007). StrengthsFinder 2.0. New York, NY: Gallup Press.

[14] Pink, D.H. (2006). A Whole New Mind: Why Right-Brainers Will Rule The Future. New York, NY: Penguin Group Inc.

[15] Gostick, A. & Christopher C. (2008). The Levity Effect: Why it Pays to Lighten Up. Hoboken, New Jersey: John Wiley & Sons Inc.

[16] Byron Reeves; J. Leighton Read. Total Engagement: Using Games and Virtual Worlds to Change the Way People Work and Businesses Compete.

[17] Patterson, K., Switzler, A., McMillan, R., Grenny, J. & Maxfield, D. (2011). Change Anything: The New Science of Personal Success. Hachette Book Group.

[18] Shahar, T. (2009). The Pursuit of Perfect: How To Stop Chasing Perfection and Start Living a Richer, Happier Life. New York, NY: McGraw Hill.

[20] Ferriss, T. (2009). The 4-Hour Workweek, Expanded and Updated: Expanded and Updated, With Over 100 New Pages of Cutting-Edge Content. New York, NY: Crown Publishers.

[21] Haidt, J. (2006). The Happiness Hypothesis: Finding Modern Truth In Ancient Wisdom. New York, NY: Sterling.

Chapter 9

[1] Patterson, K., Grenny, J., Maxfield, D., McMillan, R. & Switzler, A. (2011). Change Anything: The New Science of Personal Success. New York, NY: Hachette Book Group.

[2] James, W. (1962). Talks to Teachers on Psychology and to Students on Some of Life's Ideals. Mineola, NY: Dover Publications.

[3] Lyubomirsky, S. (2008). The How Of Happiness: A Scientific Approach To Getting The Life You Want. New York, NY: The Penguin Press.

[4] Diener, E. & Bisaws-Diener, R. (2008). Happiness: Unlocking The Mysteries of Psychological Wealth. Malden, MA: Blackwell Publishing.

[5] Baumeister, R.F., Gailliot, M., DeWall, C.N., & Oaten, M. (2006). Self-Regulation and Personality: How Interventions Increase Regulatory Success, and How Depletion Moderates the Effects of Traits on Behavior. Journal of Personality, 74, 1773-1801.

[6,7] Medina, J. (2008). Brain Rules: 12 Principles for Surviving and Thriving at Work, Home and School. Seattle, WA: Pear Press.

[8,9,13] Doidge, N. (2007) The Brain That Changes Itself: Tales of Personal Triumph from the Frontiers of Brain Science. New York, NY: Penguin.

[10] Langer, Ellen J. (2007). On Becoming an Artist: Reinventing Yourself Through Mindful Creativity. New York, NY: Ballantine Books.

[11] Ben Shahar, T. (2007). Happier: Learn the Secrets to Daily Joy and Lasting Fulfillment. New York, NY: McGraw Hill.

[12] Loehr, J. & Schwartz,T. (2003). The Power Of Full Engagement: Managing Energy, Not Time, Is the Key to High Performance and Personal Renewal. New York, NY: The Free Press.

[14] Miller, C.A. & Frisch, M.B. (2010). Creating Your Best Life: The Ultimate Life List Guide. New York, NY: Sterling.

[15, 16, 17] Haidt, J. (2006). The Happiness Hypothesis: Finding Modern Truth In Ancient Wisdom. New York, NY: Sterling.

Chapter 10

[1] Nietzsche, F. (1990). Twilight of the Idols: Or How to Philosophize with a Hammer. London: Penguin Classics.

[2, 4, 5, 16, 20, 33] Sutton, Robert I. (2010). Good Boss, Bad Boss: How to Be the Best... and Learn from the Worst. New York, NY: Hachette Book Group.

[3] (February 12, 2012) "Travel giant gets sued over bullying allegations." The Age. Retrieved at http://www.theage.com.au/business/travel-giant-gets-sued-over-bullying-allegations-20120212-1szph.html.

[6] (February 5, 2010) "Warning came too late for bullied Brodie." The Age. Retrieved at http://www.theage.com.au/national/warning-came-too-late-for-bullied-brodie-20100205-nipb.html.

[7] Zimbardo, P.G. (2008) The Lucifer Effect: Understanding How Good People Turn Evil. New York, NY: Random House.

[8] Campbell, J. (2008) The Hero with a Thousand Faces: The Collected Words of Joseph Campbell. Novato, California: New World Library.

[9, 10] (August 17, 2004) Bullied workers suffer "battle stress". BBC News Online. http://news.bbc.co.uk/2/hi/business/3563450.stm.

[11, 12] Kichin, D. (2005). Post-Traumatic Stress Disorder: The Invisible Injury. London, United Kingdom: Success Unlimited.

[13] Seligman, M.E.P (2011). Flourish: A Visionary New Understanding of Happiness and Well-being. New York, NY: Free Press.

[14, 15] Lyubomirsky, S. (2008). The How Of Happiness: A Scientific Approach To Getting The Life You Want. New York, NY: The Penguin Press.

[17] Spreitzer, G. & Porath, C. (2012). Creating Sustainable Performance. Harvard Business Review, January – February 2012, 92.

[18] Diener, E. & Biswas-Diener, R. (2008). Happiness: Unlocking The Mysteries of Psychological Wealth. Malden, MA: Blackwell Publishing.

[19, 22, 25, 28, 31, 35] Achor, S. (2010). The Happiness Advantage: The Seven Principles of Positive Psychology That Fuel Success and Performance at Work. New York, NY: Crown Publishing.

[21] Sutton. R.I. (2007). The No Assholes Rule: Building A Civilized Workplace And Surviving One That Isn't. New York, NY: Hachette Books.

[23] Losada, M., & Heaphy, E. (2004). The Role of Positivity and Connectivity in the Performance of Business Teams: A Nonlinear Dynamics Model. American Psychologist Vol. 60, p. 678-86.

[24] Fredrickson, B. (2009). Positivity: Groundbreaking Research Reveals How To Embrace The Hidden Strength of Positive Emotions, Overcome Negativity, and Thrive. New York, NY: Crown Publishers.

[26, 32] Gostick, A. & Christopher C. (2008). The Levity Effect: Why it Pays to Lighten Up. Hoboken, New Jersey: John Wiley & Sons Inc.

[27, 28] Rath, T. (2007). StrengthsFinder 2.0. New York, NY: Gallup Press.

[29] Wrzesniewski, A., & Dutton, J.E. (2010). Crafting a job: Revisioning employees as active crafters of their work. Academy of Management Review 26(2), 179-201.

[30] Haidt, J. (2006). The Happiness Hypothesis: Finding Modern Truth In Ancient Wisdom. New York, NY: Sterling.

[34] (October 11, 2007) "Many Employees Would Fire Their Boss." Gallup Management Journal. Retrieved February 21, 2012 http://gmj. gallup.com/content/28867/Many-Employees-Would-Fire-Their-Boss.aspx.

With Heartfelt Thanks

I have been blessed to work in amazing organizations with incredible bosses throughout my career. Some of these people in particular inspired me, challenged me and cheered me on so that I could go places I never dreamed possible. To Megan Dalla-Camina, Liz Merrick, Don Munro, Luke Sayers, Peter Tanner, Paul Brasher, Jim Stynes and Paul Currie I owe a huge debt of thanks for showing me what leadership looks like at its best. But perhaps the boss who most changed my life was Gene Donnelly. Not only did Gene quite literally put the world at my feet, but as a true visionary he believed strongly enough in the importance of employee well-being as a means of driving bottom line business results that he made my studies in positive psychology possible. Without his faith and trust, this book would never have been achieved.

I've also been incredibly fortunate to have wonderful team members who have provided honest feedback, encouragement and coaching to help me learn how to be a better boss – of course, there's always room for improvement! Special thanks to Manuela Schmid, Sonya Domanski, Jacqui Rivett, Fritha Ryan, Trudy Morrison and Lynne Jacobs who have become dear friends long after the job was done.

I frequently experience moments of having to pinch myself to realize how lucky I've been to have the chance to learn from the incredible scientists mentioned throughout this book. Sincere thanks to Barbara Fredrickson, Karen Reivich, Sonja Lyubomirsky, Ed Diener, George Vaillant, Shawn Achor, Mike Czsentmihalyi, Tal Ben-Shahar and Carol Dweck for your dedication to discovering the best in human life and your generosity in teaching and sharing it. Very special thanks of course to my dear professor Martin Seligman for having the courage to create the field of study and for sponsoring courses like the Masters of Applied Positive Psychology (MAPP) where people like me can have their lives transformed. Most especially, thank you Marty for your ongoing guidance, encouragement and generosity.

When I started this process I had no idea how to write a book, or make it available to the world, so huge thanks to Rachael Bermingham and the team at

159

Bermingham Books for helping to take my dream and make it a reality. Without you Rach, this book would never have existed. You made writing this a joyful experience and together I hope there may be many more.

For my family and friends who urged me to start writing, waited patiently for it to be done and celebrated the completion of this book, "thank you" doesn't even seem to come close to the gratitude I feel for having you in my life. To Kym Ridgway, Kristy Henderson and Bridget and Jimmy Purcell, thank you for the inspiration, courage and confidence. To Megan Dalla-Camina, I owe a huge vodka cocktail at a sushi bar in New York where this amazing journey started – thank you, my dear friend, I can't imagine life without you in it. To Bobby Dauman, I promise to get right back to our PhD studies and keep playing the rest of our lives. To my mum, Barb Ridgway, thank you for cheering me on.

Most importantly of all though, to my dear husband Patrick McQuaid and our two amazing sons, Charlie and Jamie, thank you for your continued support for my crazy adventures. I promise together we'll make the world a better place.

About the Author

Michelle McQuaid is a proven expert in bringing out the best in people at work. Through her videos, books, training programs and games, she's helped thousands of people to leverage their strengths, challenge their beliefs, build their resilience, create great relationships and smash through their goals at work. She prides herself on helping people to make work more rewarding and her blend of real-world successes, actionable advice and enthusiasm for life ensures Michelle is a favorite with audiences worldwide.

Michelle's ridden the dot-com wave of start-ups, been the youngest general manager ever appointed to one of the world's largest advertising houses and climbed to the top of some of the largest corporate ladders in Australia, London and New York before jumping from these giddy heights to contract on her own. Along the way, she was given the incredibly lucky break of completing her Masters in Applied Positive Psychology with Martin Seligman (the founder of this field) and is currently completing her PhD with David Cooperrider (the founder of Appreciative Inquiry).

A massive advocate for empowering people to steer their own course, Michelle's also occasionally convinced organizations like PricewaterhouseCoopers, BHP Billiton and the National Australia Bank to help design this kind of change from the top down. She also has a strong belief in paying it forward so it's her great pleasure to serve on the board of non-profit organizations like Reach (which helps build self-belief in teenagers) and Play for Life (which uses play to initiate social change projects) and partner with schools implementing positive education approaches.

With a playful, proven approach, Michelle fuses positive psychology, neuroscience and purposeful games (yes, even including the crudely termed "gamification") into simple, practical actions which anyone can take to create positive changes that last – be it bottom-up one person at a time or top-down across an entire workplace.

Michelle's currently based by the beach in Melbourne where she lives with her incredibly patient husband and their two remarkable boys who constantly bring out the best in her.

Learn more about Michelle's adventures and services at **http://www. michellemcquaid.com**.

Made in the USA
Lexington, KY
18 October 2012